NATIONAL ACADEMIES Sciences Engineering Medicine

I0794294

NATIONAL ACADEMIES PRESS
Washington, DC

Building Defense Research Capacity at Historically Black Colleges and Universities, Tribal Colleges and Universities, and Minority-Serving Institutions

André Porter and Paula Whitacre,
Rapporteurs

Board on Higher Education
and Workforce

Policy and Global Affairs

Proceedings of Three Town Halls

NATIONAL ACADEMIES PRESS 500 Fifth Street, NW Washington, DC 20001

This activity was supported by contracts between the National Academy of Sciences and the Department of Defense (W911NF-18-D-0002/W911NF-20-F-0016). Any opinions, findings, conclusions, or recommendations expressed in this publication do not necessarily reflect the views of any organization or agency that provided support for the project.

International Standard Book Number-13: 978-0-309-71609-3
International Standard Book Number-10: 0-309-71609-8
Digital Object Identifier: https://doi.org/10.17226/27511

This publication is available from the National Academies Press, 500 Fifth Street, NW, Keck 360, Washington, DC 20001; (800) 624-6242 or (202) 334-3313; http://www.nap.edu.

Printed in the United States of America.

Suggested citation: National Academies of Sciences, Engineering, and Medicine. 2024. *Building Defense Research Capacity at Historically Black Colleges and Universities, Tribal Colleges and Universities, and Minority-Serving Institutions: Proceedings of Three Town Halls*. Washington, DC: The National Academies Press. https://doi.org/10.17226/27511.

The **National Academy of Sciences** was established in 1863 by an Act of Congress, signed by President Lincoln, as a private, nongovernmental institution to advise the nation on issues related to science and technology. Members are elected by their peers for outstanding contributions to research. Dr. Marcia McNutt is president.

The **National Academy of Engineering** was established in 1964 under the charter of the National Academy of Sciences to bring the practices of engineering to advising the nation. Members are elected by their peers for extraordinary contributions to engineering. Dr. John L. Anderson is president.

The **National Academy of Medicine** (formerly the Institute of Medicine) was established in 1970 under the charter of the National Academy of Sciences to advise the nation on medical and health issues. Members are elected by their peers for distinguished contributions to medicine and health. Dr. Victor J. Dzau is president.

The three Academies work together as the **National Academies of Sciences, Engineering, and Medicine** to provide independent, objective analysis and advice to the nation and conduct other activities to solve complex problems and inform public policy decisions. The National Academies also encourage education and research, recognize outstanding contributions to knowledge, and increase public understanding in matters of science, engineering, and medicine.

Learn more about the National Academies of Sciences, Engineering, and Medicine at **www.nationalacademies.org**.

Consensus Study Reports published by the National Academies of Sciences, Engineering, and Medicine document the evidence-based consensus on the study's statement of task by an authoring committee of experts. Reports typically include findings, conclusions, and recommendations based on information gathered by the committee and the committee's deliberations. Each report has been subjected to a rigorous and independent peer-review process and it represents the position of the National Academies on the statement of task.

Proceedings published by the National Academies of Sciences, Engineering, and Medicine chronicle the presentations and discussions at a workshop, symposium, or other event convened by the National Academies. The statements and opinions contained in proceedings are those of the participants and are not endorsed by other participants, the planning committee, or the National Academies.

Rapid Expert Consultations published by the National Academies of Sciences, Engineering, and Medicine are authored by subject-matter experts on narrowly focused topics that can be supported by a body of evidence. The discussions contained in rapid expert consultations are considered those of the authors and do not contain policy recommendations. Rapid expert consultations are reviewed by the institution before release.

For information about other products and activities of the National Academies, please visit www.nationalacademies.org/about/whatwedo.

BUILDING DEFENSE RESEARCH CAPACITY AT HISTORICALLY BLACK COLLEGES AND UNIVERSITIES AND OTHER MINORITY INSTITUTIONS WORKSHOP PLANNING COMMITTEE

OSCAR BARTON, JR., Ph.D., P.E. (*Chair*), Dean, Clarence M. Mitchell, Jr., School of Engineering, Morgan State University
BRYN ADAMS, Ph.D., Branch Chief, U.S. Army DEVCOM Army Research Laboratory
MELVIN GREER, Ph.D., Intel Fellow and Chief Data Scientist, Americas, Intel Corporation
KEITH A. MCGEE, Ph.D., Associate Provost for Research, Innovation, and Graduate Education, Alcorn State University
ABIGAIL S. NEWSOME, Ph.D., Associate Vice President for Academic Affairs, Mississippi Valley State University
SHAWNÉ RAIFORD, M.B.A., Space Workforce 2030 Program Manager, DEI, The Aerospace Corporation
THOMAS C. TUBON, Ph.D., Chief Workforce Development Officer, BioMADE
ABRAHAM WOLCOTT, Ph.D., Associate Professor, Chemistry, San José State University
CHAD WOMACK, Ph.D., Senior Director of National STEM Programs and Initiatives, United Negro College Fund

Staff

ANDRÉ N. PORTER, M.S., Senior Program Officer, Board on Higher Education and Workforce
JOHN N. VERAS, Associate Program Officer, Board on Higher Education and Workforce
KARLA RILEY, Senior Program Assistant, Board on Higher Education and Workforce
MARIA LUND DAHLBERG, M.S., Director, Board on Higher Education and Workforce

Consultants

PAULA WHITACRE, Consultant Writer

Reviewers

This Proceedings of a Three Town Halls was reviewed in draft form by individuals chosen for their diverse perspectives and technical expertise. The purpose of this independent review is to provide candid and critical comments that will assist the National Academies of Sciences, Engineering, and Medicine in making each published proceedings as sound as possible and to ensure that it meets the institutional standards for quality, objectivity, evidence, and responsiveness to the charge. The review comments and draft manuscript remain confidential to protect the integrity of the process.

We thank the following individuals for their review of this proceedings:

EVY GONZALEZ, Texas State University
ANNA QUIDER, Northern Illinois University
WANDA SIGUR, Lockheed Martin Corporation

Although the reviewers listed above provided many constructive comments and suggestions, they were not asked to endorse the content of the proceedings nor did they see the final draft before its release. The review of this proceedings was overseen by **MARILYN BAKER,** National Academies of Sciences, Engineering, and Medicine. She was responsible for making certain that an independent examination of this proceedings was carried out in accordance with standards of the National Academies and that all review comments were carefully considered. Responsibility for the final content rests entirely with the rapporteurs and the National Academies.

Preface

Minority institutions with programs that develop and supply talent for the science, technology engineering and mathematics (STEM) workforce pipeline have a major impact on its readiness across all industry sectors: public and private, for-profit and not-for-profit, and military and government. Minority institutions, too, have been engines of innovation contributing to each industrial revolution with purpose and conviction. While these institutions have mostly capitalized on government, private, and philanthropic resources to build their research enterprises, increasing participation in Department of Defense research offers tremendous promise to expand capacity but also meet the challenges of the 21st century war fighter. The outcome of this work is intended to reveal strategies to do so.

Through a series of town halls, offered at locations nationwide, the planning committee brought together academics, subject matter experts, administrators, and industry leaders for open, actionable conversations on two themes: building true partnerships and identifying barriers to establishing and/or enhancing research capacity at minority institutions. Held in Washington, DC, the first town hall included highlights of the defense research and development environment, shared strategies for articulating the value proposition for partnership development, outlined defense industry criteria for developing partnerships with academic institutions, and surveyed historic and current models for the development of synergistic partnerships. The second town hall was held in Albuquerque, New Mexico, and looked intra-institutionally to address barriers. Topics included understanding the impact of the faculty workload policy and infrastructure investments on research productivity. In addition, the participants discussed barriers that hampered capacity-building activities and shared strategies for developing diverse research portfolios. The final town hall examined approaches to elevate an institution's research activity, offered targeted strategies to recruit for research-centered faculty, and identified supportive administrative structures to enhance productivity. The town hall was held in Chicago, Illinois.

Moderated panel sessions with invited stakeholders and constituents representative from government, private sector, academia, and community organization was the structured approach adopted to collect inputs. Participants were given an opportunity to provide opening remarks or give short presentations prior to engaging in a question-and-answer period. This effort would not have been possible without the selfless participation of the organizing committee to include Dr. Abraham Wilcott, San Jose State University; Dr. Melvin Greer, Intel Corporation; Dr. Thomas Tubon, BioMADE; Dr. Abigail Newsome, Mississippi Valley State University; Dr. Chad Womack, United Negro College Fund; and Dr. Keith McGee. I thank each of you for sharing passion while working on this project.

It goes without saying, but I must, that the work would not have reached completion without the dedication and experience of the National Academies staff. André Porter, who provided guidance and support to the committee, was invaluable. John Veras coordinated each session to ensure each was successfully executed, and Ms. Karla Riley provided timely administrative support. Thank you all.

Oscar Barton, Jr., Ph.D., P.E.
Dean, Clarence M. Mitchell, Jr., School of Engineering
Morgan State University

Contents

Box, Figures, and Table

BOX

FIGURES

TABLE

1

Introduction

Historically Black Colleges and Universities (HBCUs), Tribal Colleges and Universities (TCUs), Hispanic-Serving Institutions (HSIs), Alaska Native and Native Hawaiian–Serving Institutions (ANNHSIs), and other Minority Institutions (MIs) represent a valuable resource to expand the Department of Defense's (DOD) science and technology workforce and research enterprise. There are more than 800 public and private 2- and 4-year Minority-Serving Institutions (MSIs) nationwide, including the U.S. territories, with many near DOD facilities.[1] Many of these institutions are already conducting cutting-edge research in areas of high priority to the U.S. government, while others could be positioned to do so with strategic investments. With their diverse population of U.S. citizens, they also offer DOD an opportunity to widen its talent pool, diversify science, technology, engineering, and mathematics (STEM) research, and ultimately strengthen national security.

Defined in the U.S. federal statute (20 U.S. Code § 1067k), "minority institution" is a specific term referring to an institution of higher education whose enrollment of a single minority or a combination of minorities

---

[1] The Rutgers Center for Minority Serving Institutions maintains a list of current MSIs across the United States, based on the U.S. Department of Education Office of Postsecondary Education's 2023 eligibility matrix. For the Rutgers Center's list of MSIs, see https://cmsi.gse.rutgers.edu/msi-directory. For the Department of Education's eligibility designations, matrix, and other MSI information, see https://www2.ed.gov/about/offices/list/ope/idues/eligibility.html.

exceeds 50 percent of the total enrollment. This is in contrast to the term "minority-serving institution." The U.S. federal statute (20 U.S. Code § 1067q) describes MSIs as institutions that range in enrollment from 10 to 40 percent of a single minority group. Discussions included in the town hall proceedings used the term minority institution to describe both federally designated MIs, such as HBCUs and TCUs, and federally designated MSIs, such as Hispanic-Serving Institutions and Asian American and Pacific Islander Serving Institutions (see Table 1-1). Speakers throughout the series used both terms interchangeably.

This proceedings uses the definitions set in the 2022 National Academies of Sciences, Engineering, and Medicine consensus study report *Defense Research Capacity at Historically Black Colleges and Universities and Other Minority Institutions: Transitioning from Good Intentions to Measurable Outcomes.* The National Defense Authorization Act for Fiscal Year 2020,[2] and subsequent federal legislation, focuses on this smaller subset of the broader group of MSIs: minority institutions. That 2022 report examines the status of DOD research at these institutions. The report examined some of the methods and means necessary to advance research capacity to comprehensively address the national security and defense needs of the United States (NASEM, 2022).

The 2022 report builds upon the foundation set by the National Academies' 2019 report *Minority Serving Institutions: America's Underutilized Resource for Strengthening the STEM Workforce*, which highlighted the ways the broader group of MSIs across the country provide pathways to STEM educational success and workforce readiness for millions of students of color—and do so in a mission-driven and intentional manner (NASEM, 2019). As the 2022 report's subtitle suggests (*Transitioning from Good Intentions to Measurable Outcomes*), DOD recognizes the potential contributions of and supports many HBCU/MI programs, but there are significant discrepancies in the amount, duration, and type of DOD funding when compared with non-HBCUs/MIs.

ORIGINS OF THE TOWN HALL SERIES

As DOD and other partners sought to implement the 2022 report's

[2] For the federal legislation, see S.1790—National Defense Authorization Act for Fiscal Year 2020. In accordance with federal statute, the subset of institutions that are accredited postsecondary minority institutions (or MIs) are maintained by the Department of Education at https://www2.ed.gov/about/offices/list/ocr/edlite-minorityinst-list-tab.html.

TABLE 1-1 Minority Institution Categories

Minority Institutions	
Historically Designated Minority Institutions	Minority-Serving Institutions
Historically Black Colleges and Universities (HBCUs)	Alaska Native and Native Hawaiian Serving Institution (ANNHSI)
Tribal Colleges and Universities (TCUs)	Asian American and Pacific Islander Serving Institution (AAPISI)
	Hispanic-Serving Institution (HSI)
	Native American-Serving Non-Tribal Institution (NMSNTI)
	Predominantly Black Institution (PBI)

recommendations, key questions remained to be explored, particularly related to how to seek ways of building research capacity at MIs and develop true partnerships between MIs, other institutions of higher education, and federal agencies. To consider these questions and related issues, the DOD HBCU/MI Program and Outreach Office of the Under Secretary for Research and Engineering asked the National Academies to hold a series of workshops in a town hall format. The 2022 report provided key recommendations to the Under Secretary of Defense for Research and Engineering to work with the military departments, defense agencies, and institutions of higher education to support MI defense-related research capacity, as well as foster *true* partnerships: "those that are mutually beneficial and grounded in mutual respect, meaningful engagement, and equity in funding and resources—can present opportunities for joint research and collaboration, workforce development, and transition and commercialization, and can help HBCU/MIs build and advance their own capacity to conduct DOD-funded research" (NASEM, 2022).

In early 2023, the National Academies convened a nine-member committee of STEM professionals across sectors and disciplines to develop this series of three workshops. (See Box 1-1 for the Statement of Task.) The workshops were held in a hybrid format in Washington, DC (April 24–25,

2023), Albuquerque, New Mexico (May 22–23, 2023), and Chicago, Illinois (June 28–29, 2023).

ORGANIZATION OF THIS PROCEEDINGS

The remainder of this publication is organized to follow the agenda of the three town halls. Chapters 2 and 3 cover the first town hall, which focused on capacity development, including faculty policies, culture and leadership models, and investments. The first town hall explored barriers that dissuade capacity building at MIs, investigated faculty workload policies, explored research portfolio diversification, and spotlighted models used across the federal government to support research capacity development at underresourced higher education institutions. Chapters 4 and 5 focus on the second town hall, which looked at partnerships and presented the benefits of true partnerships to DOD, the challenges to development of partnerships, and a range of successful institutional and federal agency models. This town hall provided an overview of the defense research and development landscape and illustrated strategies for articulating the value proposition for partnership development. Speakers outlined defense industry criteria for developing partnerships with academic institutions and spotlighted models for developing synergistic partnerships, with representatives from academia, the defense industry, and federal programs that seek to facilitate equitable government-university-industry partnerships.

The third town hall, summarized in Chapters 6 and 7, looked at how to transition from low to high research activity through faculty recruitment and retention, administrative capacity, and other factors. In this final town hall, the committee and staff sought to evaluate the components necessary to elevate an institution's research activity, highlighting support structures for research faculty and personnel and possible recruitment strategies to draw in research-centered faculty at MIs. The final town hall featured a recapitulation of the topics, programs, and institutions featured throughout the whole series with spotlights on strategies and best practices used at academic institutions to increase research capacity building and foster equitable research partnerships.

In sum, each town hall featured presentations by a variety of thought partners about successful programs for students, faculty, and/or institutions. The workshop series featured higher education programs and MIs with successful models and the problems and barriers they have encountered in

BOX 1-1
Statement of Task

A planning committee of the National Academies of Sciences, Engineering, and Medicine will organize and host a series of three hybrid workshops to examine the key issues highlighted in the National Academies' consensus study report, *Defense Research Capacity at Historically Black Colleges and Universities and Other Minority Institutions: Transitioning from Good Intentions to Measurable Outcomes* (2022). The workshops will feature commissioned research and literature reviews as well as "case studies" to illuminate problems, barriers, and approaches to increase research capacity, (e.g., programs and initiatives at HBCUs [Historically Black Colleges and Universities], TCUs [Tribal Colleges and Universities], HSIs [Hispanic-Serving Institutions], and other minority-serving institutions; programs and initiatives that span departments or institutions or include other sectors; and programs and initiatives supported by DOD [Department of Defense] and other government agencies). Workshop topics will include

True Partnerships

- What are common barriers that dissuade research and educational partnerships and collaborations that are truly beneficial for all partners, especially the HBCUs, TCUs, HSIs, and other minority-serving institutions' partners?
- How can DOD facilitate equitable research and educational partnerships and collaborations through the use of existing and the development of new incentives?
- What short- and long-term actions can DOD take to facilitate the development, maintenance, renegotiation, and revision of mutually beneficial research and educational partnerships and collaborations?

Building Research Capacity

- What specific challenges do HBCUs, TCUs, HSIs, and other minority-serving institutions encounter in developing their defense-related research capacity?
- How can DOD and other government agencies facilitate the adaptation of defense-related research capacity programs or policies from Primarily White Universities and HBCUs, TCUs, HSIs, and other minority-serving institutions?
- What short- and long-term actions can DOD and other government agencies take to support and engage HBCUs, TCUs, HSIs, and other minority-serving institutions in the development of new or additional defense-related research capacity?

their efforts to increase MI defense-related research. Additionally, federal agency representatives shared their thoughts and programs of note to support MIs. The featured programs and institutional efforts provide brief case studies for MIs, DOD, and other government agencies to consider in their engagement with MIs. The workshop series did not feature commissioned research (conducted by researchers outside the National Academies staff or the committee), as the workshop committee and staff believed the range of programs, institutions, speakers, and topics featured across the workshop series provide the latest research to illuminate problems, barriers, and approaches to increase research capacity at these crucial institutions. A commissioned paper will be published separately from this proceedings as a supplemental document.

The town hall agendas and biographical sketches of the speakers can be found in Appendixes A and B, respectively. In accordance with the policies of the National Academies, workshop participants did not attempt to establish any conclusions or recommendations about needs and future directions, focusing instead on issues discussed by the speakers and workshop participants. In addition, the planning committee's role was limited to planning the workshop. This proceedings was prepared by a rapporteur as a factual summary of what occurred at the workshop.

REFERENCES

NASEM (National Academies of Sciences, Engineering, and Medicine). 2019. *Minority Serving Institutions: America's Underutilized Resource for Strengthening the STEM Workforce.* Washington, DC: The National Academies Press.

NASEM. 2022. *Defense Research Capacity at Historically Black Colleges and Universities and Other Minority Institutions: Transitioning from Good Intentions to Measurable Outcomes.* Washington, DC: The National Academies Press.

2

Town Hall I, Day 1: Capacity Development in Institutions, Policies, and Culture and Leadership Models

Highlights from the Presentations

- Tribal Colleges and Universities offer DOD and federal agencies unique perspectives and knowledge that can provide strategic value in such areas as environmental science and health, agriculture, climate change adaptation, and other areas to build national security (Christelle, Biggane, Kuslikis).
- Hispanic-Serving Institutions, including large institutions like Texas A&M and those in the California State University system, provide undergraduate and graduate students with meaningful research opportunities that can lead to defense-related research and employment, but many students are not aware of the opportunities (Butler-Purry, Gomez, Erogbogbo).
- To allow faculty more time for research, institutions can reduce extra tasks, make use of postdocs, and take advantage of expertise in the surrounding areas and communities to find contingent faculty to relieve teaching loads (Crockett).
- Starting small and building over time may result in the successful establishment of sustainable research centers. These kinds of programs can expand impact because they attract students, faculty, and others (Sankar).

- Unless TCUs are explicitly mentioned in an opportunity for Minority-Serving Institutions, they tend not to be included, in part because of their smaller total numbers, yet they offer thousands of years of knowledge in key areas (Baker).

This list is the rapporteurs' summary of points made by the individual speakers identified, and the statements have not been endorsed or verified by the National Academies of Sciences, Engineering, and Medicine. They are not intended to reflect a consensus among workshop participants.

Committee chair Oscar Barton, Jr., Ph.D., P.E. (Morgan State University), welcomed participants to the first of three town halls to uncover topics that can advance research at Historically Black Colleges and Universities (HBCUs), Tribal Colleges and Universities (TCUs), Hispanic-Serving Institutions (HSIs), and Alaska Native and Native Hawaiian–Serving Institutions (ANNHSIs) supported by the Department of Defense (DOD) and other agencies. The entire town hall series, he explained, was designed to identify barriers that are hindering advancement but, more importantly, to highlight policies and procedures to advance capacity, including through case studies, and to discuss infrastructure and capacity.

BUILDING DEFENSE-RELATED RESEARCH CAPACITY AT MINORITY INSTITUTIONS

The session began with perspectives from leaders at each set of institutions: HBCUs, TCUs, HSIs, and ANNHSIs. They spoke about their institutions' research goals and the steps they are taking to achieve them through policies, procedures, and operations. The institutions discussed barriers, challenges, and opportunities in their efforts.

Historically Black Colleges and Universities

Providing a perspective from two HBCUs were John Anderson, Ph.D. (Howard University), and Farin Kamangar, M.D., Ph.D. (Morgan State University).

Howard University

The U.S. Air Force designated Howard University as a University Affiliated Research Center (UARC) in tactical autonomy in early 2023, the first HBCU to lead a UARC.[1] With this great opportunity comes great responsibility, Dr. Anderson commented. Howard's president and other senior leaders have been engaged in the planning "because it's so important we get this right."

In response to Dr. Barton's question about goals, Dr. Anderson shared both university and college or department-specific goals. Success in faculty research involves very specific strategies, for example, in bringing postdocs on board. Faculty want to execute their research with as little stress as possible in terms of administration and management; thus, it is important to understand how to best serve them in an efficient way that allows them to submit and execute grants and contracts. In response to the increased funded research, Dr. Anderson noted an institutional need for the infrastructure to support this research. Howard has been seeking and receiving larger grants and contracts, as opposed to the smaller, individual grants that composed most of its research activity in the past. Center grants and the UARC will require finding and hiring individuals with the knowledge and skills to support this transformation. He noted a tight labor market for this type of expertise.

Morgan State University

Dr. Kamangar spoke of internal and external barriers to growing research capacity and how Morgan State University is addressing them. In 2022, Morgan State received new funding commitments of about $75 million from DOD, as well as awards from NASA, National Institutes of Health (NIH), and National Science Foundation (NSF). Within the past year, DOD awarded Morgan State $7.5 million for its Center for 2D Materials and $9 million for Equitable Artificial Intelligence.[2,3]

Reviewing overall U.S. research and development (R&D) funding (Congressional Research Service, 2022), Dr. Kamangar pointed out that

[1] For more information about the UARC at Howard University, see https://www.defense.gov/News/News-Stories/Article/Article/3275321/howard-university-will-be-lead-institution-for-new-research-center/.

[2] For more information, see https://www.morgan.edu/physics/dodcenter.

[3] For more information, see https://www.morgan.edu/ceamls.

DOD awards a large portion of the $160 billion R&D federal total; he urged more be directed to minority-serving institutions. External barriers include clauses in the Federal Acquisition Regulations, or FAR, that are sometimes unnecessarily included in contracts. Other barriers he cited are prohibitions on publication (which faculty need for promotion and tenure); export controls that are unclear in terms of the nature of the research; IDIQ (Indefinite Delivery, Indefinite Quantity) contracts in which major partners apportion only a small amount of the total to HBCUs; incorrect assumptions about HBCU faculty capabilities; time and material contracts that are incompatible with existing HBCU reporting or accounting systems; and less likelihood that HBCUs are involved when proposals are envisioned. Internal barriers include a lack of belief that the institution can win a large award, although this perception has decreased; inadequate training for contracting staff; and inadequate computing or other infrastructure.

One hundred years ago, Dr. Kamangar related, Morgan State was a small teaching institution with a single building and has grown to a sprawling research campus. Pioneering research in the 1960s was mostly unfunded. As Dr. Anderson described for Howard, funded research is increasing and infrastructure must be built. Morgan State now has an R2 research designation under the Carnegie Classification of Institutions of Higher Education, and the goal is R1 designation.[4] To help achieve this, Morgan State University president David Wilson, Ed.D., established the Division of Research and Economic Development, with Willie May, Ph.D., as vice president for research. Within this division, the Office of Research Administration provides resources and training to faculty, with improvement over the past 5 years but still more work to do, Dr. Kamangar said. An Office of Technology Transfer and Intellectual Property has also been strengthened. Starting in 2016, six research centers have been established with stable funding. Three in particular are related to DOD: the Cybersecurity Assurance and Policy Center, Center for Equitable AI and Machine Learning Systems, and Center for Education and Research in Microelectronics.

Dr. Kamangar thanked DOD colleagues who have visited the campus but stressed the importance of creating more opportunities for HBCUs. He suggested more seminars for HBCUs on DOD opportunities and

---

[4] For more information about the Carnegie Classification of Institutions of Higher Education, see https://carnegieclassifications.acenet.edu/.

more visits by DOD staff to HBCU campuses to speak with principal investigators (PIs). Training and funding for contracting offices, similar to those at NIH and NSF, would also be helpful, he suggested. Some larger institutions, he observed, have been doing this work since the 1940s and have developed capacity over time. With the growing number of laws and paperwork, training matters. He also noted that major partners sometimes include an HBCU on a proposal to win an award and then the HBCU receives only a small portion of the funding, and he urged a requirement that a certain percentage be directed to the HBCU partner.

Discussion

Dr. Barton asked the presenters about the relationship between execution of contracts and their institutions' legal offices. Dr. Anderson said that with larger grants, and executing or receiving subcontracts, it is critical that the Office of General Counsel (OGC) work well with research teams to begin implementation as quickly as possible. Once an award has been made, "the clock is running, and the PI immediately feels a sense of stress when they are managing a large contract or grant." A dean does not have a direct impact on contractual issues, but it is important to emphasize to the provost and other leaders the importance to the mission of the university. Dr. Kamangar echoed the importance of strong working relationships with the OGC to strengthen contracting processes. At Morgan State, the OGC provided parameters to contracting officers to conduct some independent reviews within the Office of Research. He also called attention to a UC2 mechanism out of the National Cancer Institute to support a grants office and to NIH's Support of Competitive Research (SCORE) program.[5] He expressed hope that DOD would consider such grants to enhance research infrastructure to meet DOD needs.

Dr. Barton underscored that in addition to building physical capacity, HBCUs and other Minority-Serving Institutions (MSIs) must build human capacity to conduct research and execute grants and contracts. He agreed with the need to be fairly treated as a sub-awardee. He also noted that many HBCUs began with a mission of teaching and are evolving to a new mission overlaid around research. It is a form of mission creep, he commented,

[5] *UC2* is a National Institutes of Health grant activity code for "High Impact Research and Research Infrastructure Cooperative Agreement Programs"; for more information, see https://grants.nih.gov/grants/funding/ac_search_results.htm. For more information on SCORE, see https://grants.nih.gov/grants/guide/pa-files/par-20-039.html.

in that they are expected to maintain core experiences but also bring on research. He concluded with a reflection that initiatives from other agencies may be helpful to consider for DOD-related research.

Tribal Colleges and Universities

Committee member Abraham Wolcott, Ph.D. (San José State University), moderated a panel comprising Andrea Christelle, Ph.D. (Diné College), Emily Biggane, Ph.D. (United Tribes Technical College [UTTC]), and Al Kuslikis (American Indian Higher Education Consortium [AIHEC]).

Diné College

Before coming to Diné College, Dr. Christelle worked at the University of Texas at Austin. Seeing the huge difference in resources between the two institutions, she commented, "gives us pause to think about what has been made possible by historic investment." She welcomed DOD interest in moving from good intentions to measurable outcomes, as noted in the 2022 National Academies consensus study report.

Diné, which was founded as Navajo Community College in 1968, began offering 4-year degrees about 5 years ago and is now transitioning to a research university with Dr. Christelle as the first vice president of research. As the college of the Navajo Nation, which is about the size of the state of West Virginia, Diné has a main campus and several smaller campuses that serve as community resource centers. Dr. Christelle's unit is called Na'al Kaah Bee Honít'I', or Research, Innovation and Practice. "We explicitly use the Diné language, because it focuses on the different epistemic framework and knowledge creation that is possible through Diné College," she explained.

In supporting the institution, she said, it is important to emphasize not only the opportunity to address historic injustices but also the strategic advantages and unique thinking that can benefit DOD and other agencies. Examples include the Navajo Code Talkers of World War II and knowledge in traditional lifeways and agriculture that has implications for global security in a warming world. Diné's educational philosophy of thinking creatively, planning, enacting, and reflecting embodies a conception of circular time, in contrast to the more linear time frame of Western thinking with a definite beginning and end. "The ability to bring this perspective, and to create and explore from this unique epistemic perspective, has real value," she said. "We want to make the case that we have something strategic to offer."

Economic and infrastructure development is a real need, given that 30 percent of homes in the Navajo Nation lack electricity and plumbing. Thus, a focus of Diné College's research activity is technology transfer. It was the first TCU to secure a patent (for a sensor used in epilepsy testing) and received congressional funding to build a technology transfer center for scientific innovation and for the protection of intellectual property rights of Navajo artisans. The National Telecommunications and Information Administration awarded Diné a grant (Connect Navajo) to build out research infrastructure, acquire hardware, and train information technology staff. The Mellon Foundation is supporting a program in which Navajo people working outside the nation come to campus to share their expertise with students. Diné has also received GRANTED (Growing Research Access for Nationally Transformative Equity and Diversity) funding from the National Science Foundation to build its research administration staff (see Chapter 3 for more information on this NSF program). They have aligned staff positions with the needs of the field (pre-award coordinator, post-award coordinator, director of sponsored projects) and are developing networks with research administrators at Arizona State University, Northern Arizona University, and the University of Arizona. For the first time, summer seed funding is available for faculty to develop projects, with the help of Dr. Christelle's office, and to look for follow-on funding.

Future priorities are to build research administration capacity and to move from short- to long-form F&A (facilities and administration). She commented that the structure of F&A is such that it benefits institutions that have had historic investments and works against those that have not. The short-term goal is increasing competitive federal funding from $8 million to $10 million, which would enable them to apply for long-form F&A, and, in the longer term, to reach $50 million. A University of Arizona mentor is aiding in building out the research infrastructure and developing strategies for Diné to serve as the prime recipient of a grant or contract, and not always a sub-awardee.

United Tribes Technical College

Dr. Biggane discussed research capacity at United Tribes Technical College, which was founded in 1969 and has been accredited since 1982 by the Higher Learning Commission. It has educated more than 10,000 American Indian students from more than 75 tribes. The college is governed by the five tribes of North Dakota and offers four bachelor of science degrees among its programs. In 2018, UTTC received an NSF award to establish an Intertribal Research and Resource Center with a focus on food, water, and energy sustainability.

Dr. Biggane identified challenges and opportunities in four main areas. The first area related to faculty capacity. Faculty teach a minimum of 30 credit hours, although most teach more than that, and it is difficult to provide release time. There are not extra faculty to pick up courses, and it is hard to bring in adjuncts. Opportunities include collaborative strategies and funding for research-focused faculty. She also suggested that TCU-connected internships could provide a way for students to stay at their home institutions and participate in meaningful internships.

The second area related to expertise and interest. Faculty are often unclear of the overlap between their expertise and DOD research needs. In addition, students seek research and other experiences that benefit their communities. Opportunities are to increase awareness through workshops and small lunch-and-learn sessions so that there is a familiar face with whom to connect at DOD and other agencies. She echoed Dr. Christelle about the advantage to DOD of collaborative development and bringing Indigenous perspectives and knowledge to the table. She urged continued efforts to diversify the workforce, noting how helpful it is for students to see role models who look like them in science, technology, engineering, and mathematics (STEM) positions to promote self-confidence and a sense of belonging.

A third area with both challenges and opportunities relates to infrastructure. UTTC has a new science and technology building but is quickly outgrowing it. The IT department employs only four or five people, with no storage or management for large datasets. Opportunities include funding to expand physical and computer facilities. She noted AIHEC has an effort to expand physical server capacity across TCUs.

Finally, Dr. Biggane discussed the need for equitable partnerships. She noted that, instead, TCUs are treated as an "afterthought," which is a barrier to developing equitable partnerships. "This produces challenges because there is an extremely short turnaround to get information back to partners, and it also limits the intellectual investment we can put in." She criticized when UTTC or other TCUs are only a "participatory check box," in which an RFP (Request for Proposal) requires a larger institution to partner with a TCU, and the institution looks for the easiest one to contract but that may not be the best fit. "If you engage with us early, we do have good ideas and skill sets. We can collaborate to minimize challenges. Collaborative relationships are the most successful, but they take a while to develop to be successful," she concluded.

American Indian Higher Education Consortium

Mr. Kuslikis noted that Dr. Christelle and Dr. Biggane laid out the challenges and opportunities at their TCUs, and he would expand the conversation to discuss how TCUs and other smaller MSIs can strengthen the DOD research ecosystem. He first explained that AIHEC was established by TCUs 50 years ago. There are now 35 TCUs represented by 230 federally recognized tribes, and two additional institutions are being developed.

AIHEC has a STEM vision statement to build a framework of strategic partnerships, resources, and tools that will strengthen TCUs and their communities in STEM and to ensure American Indian students achieve success in STEM research and careers. Research in such areas as environmental science and environmental health fill a need in tribal communities, he stressed. He pointed to an overlap of strategic priorities between DOD and TCUs (see Figure 2-1). Mr. Kuslikis noted the "emerging technologies" highlighted by the Office of the Under Secretary of Defense for Research and Engineering [OUSD(R&E)], and the "effective adoption areas" for "robust private-sector activity."[6] In his presentation, Figure 2-1 illustrates the overlap of DOD technology priorities and tribal nation-relevant priorities. Examples include decision-making tools, environmental monitoring, and artificial intelligence (AI). While some fields require a higher level of technology than currently exists at most TCUs, he suggested using these priority areas to direct a long-term view for TCUs to put students on the pathway to research careers.

Every institution has a role to build partnerships with federal agencies within the larger innovation ecosystem, Mr. Kuslikis stressed. In considering how to build relationships, he explained the "six Rs" of Indigenous research—Respect, Relevance, Reciprocity, Responsibility, Representation,

---

[6] These "emerging technologies" and "effective adoption areas" were highlighted in the 2022 National Defense Science and Technology strategy led by OUSD(R&E). For the February 1, 2022, letter by Under Secretary of Defense for Research and Engineering Heidi Shyu, see https://www.cto.mil/wp-content/uploads/2022/02/usdre_strategic_vision_critical_tech_areas.pdf.

DoD Technology Priorities	**Tribal Nation-Relevant Priorities**
Emerging Technologies • **Biotechnology** • **Quantum Science** • **Future Generation Wireless Technology (FutureG)** • **Advanced Materials** ***Robust Private Sector Activity*** • **Integrated Network Systems of Systems** • **Renewable Energy Generation and Storage** • **Advanced Computing and Software** • **Human-Machine Interfaces**	• **Climate Resilience: Food, Water Security** • **Energy Sovereignty** • **Data Management/Sovereignty** • **Sustainable Economies** • **Public Health/Safety** • **Language/Culture Vitality** ***Opportunities for Collaboration*** • **Health, Agricultural Applications of Biotechnologies** • **Secure Information/Communication Systems and Data Sovereignty** • **Environmental Monitoring Systems for Climate/Weather Vulnerabilities** • **Decision-Making Tools (AI, Data Analytics, Actionable Science)**

FIGURE 2-1 DOD–tribal priority linkages.
SOURCE: Al Kuslikis, Town Hall Presentation, April 24, 2023.

and Relationships. As partnerships grow across all MSIs, these principles are applicable, and it is important to explore how to incorporate them in the growing innovation ecosystem that encompasses academic programs, faculty, and institutions. Academic programs should provide a core STEM curriculum, inquiry-based learning, and student research experiences. Faculty need reduced teaching loads, professional development and mentoring, and collaborative relationships. Institutions should provide leadership support to build research programs and campus cyberinfrastructure. In his view, campus cyberinfrastructure should be a core strategy to level the planning field so that all MSIs have access and can participate in research, citing the NSF-funded Minority Serving – Cyberinfrastructure Consortium (MS-CC) as a good example.[7]

Hispanic-Serving Institutions

An overview from the perspective of HSIs was provided by Karen Butler-Purry, Ph.D. (Texas A&M University), Frank Gomez, Ph.D.

[7] For more information on MS-CC, see https://www.ms-cc.org.

(California State University [CSU] system), and Folarin Erogbogbo, Ph.D. (San José State University [SJSU]).

Texas A&M University

Texas A&M University was designated an HSI in March 2022, as more than 25 percent of its undergraduate students are Hispanic. Dr. Butler-Purry shared thoughts about involving underrepresented students in DOD research. It is a challenge to engage undergraduate students in research, many of whom lack awareness of the benefits. Many are first-generation students who cannot participate without funding. There is competition with high-paying industry jobs, internships, and other opportunities. Some students are hesitant to engage in DOD research; they may be concerned about the security clearance process or have misperceptions or lack of knowledge about the benefits of defense research.

Graduate enrollment at Texas A&M provides a different snapshot than undergraduate enrollment, with a much smaller number of in-state students, she continued. Hispanics are about 12 percent and African Americans are about 4 percent of total graduate enrollment. Challenges in engaging them in DOD research include competition from industry, especially for those who have undergraduate student loans. There are limited scholarships for master's students.

Dr. Butler-Purry's recommendations to encourage diverse undergraduates to engage in DOD research include scholarships and funds to engage in research beginning as freshmen, more summer internships at defense facilities or on campus to compete with industry, and nurturing knowledge and awareness in the opportunities. She urged DOD personnel to engage with students on campus, such as through student organizations like the National Society of Black Engineers or the Society of Hispanic Professional Engineers. From a graduate student perspective, Dr. Butler-Purry urged increased partnerships with fellowship programs, such as the GEM Fellowships or Graduate Fellowships for STEM Diversity, and student loan forgiveness opportunities, which she said some cyber programs offer.[8] She reiterated that regular engagement with DOD personnel could demystify and dispel students' misperceptions.

[8] For more information on GEM, see https://www.gemfellowship.org/gem-fellowship-program/. For more information on the Graduate Fellowships for STEM Diversity, see https://stemfellowships.org.

California State University System STEM-NET

Dr. Gomez discussed STEM-NET (Science, Technology, Engineering and Mathematics Network) within the California State University Office of the Chancellor, which works with the 23 campuses of the CSU system. He noted that CSU is the largest and most diverse university system in the United States, and most of the campuses are HSIs. There is a total of 470,000 students and 49,000 faculty and staff. Overall, California enrolls about 1.1 million Latinx students in higher education, and about 20 percent of them are at CSU campuses. One of every 19 engineering degrees in the United States is awarded from the CSU system, he said. (Representatives from several campuses also spoke during the town halls, including from San José State University, San Diego State University, and California State University, Fullerton; presented in this chapter and in Chapters 5, 6, and 7.)

The goal of STEM-NET is to create pathways for students, share resources, and share best practices for students and faculty. Over the past 3 years, STEM-NET has helped obtain 40 awards from federal agencies and private organizations, with a total of about $50 million in funding. Dr. Gomez echoed some of the previous challenges discussed, such as those related to faculty workloads and infrastructure, but he also pointed to some unique challenges. CSU relies on state funding, which varies from year to year and comes with different priorities. The leadership changes frequently, with a turnover in provost positions every 2 to 3 years, most of whom do not have STEM or research backgrounds, which may mean less synergy with faculty who want to engage in research. Diverse priorities arise because of the need to maintain or increase student enrollment, and various laws and policies affect the system. The CSU system offers very few doctoral programs and even limited master's programs; thus, research needs to involve undergraduates in alignment with the Teacher-Scholar model and "making by doing," a phrase Dr. Gomez used to refer to CSU students and faculty involved in experiential learning. However, Dr. Gomez said, "what we do have are opportunities for experiential learning through research, field experiences, internships, service learning, and other efforts." He commented that his involvement in research as a Cal State undergraduate inspired him to become a professor. Salaries at CSU institutions are below R1 and private institutions, especially when considering the high cost of living where many are located. High teaching loads and committee work limit faculty research time.

As recommendations, Dr. Gomez urged improving the partnership between DOD and across MSIs, rather than pitting different types of MSIs against each other to secure funding. Understanding is a two-way street, based on reciprocity. "What can we offer each other and serve each other's needs?" he asked. "DOD is sometimes a black box for MSI faculty, who think they have nothing to offer." But, he countered, MSIs offer a diverse student body and community-engaged research that can be tied to national needs and STEM workforce development. For example, climate change, equity, and energy are student passions and important to national security. CSU and other MSIs build whole-person or "power" skills, including such human-centered skills as critical thinking and team building. He suggested looking at NSF for ideas in developing student training and campus systemic cultural change, including programs in the new Directorate for Technology, Innovation, and Partnerships (see Chapter 5). He also suggested a joint HSI-HBCU-TCU R1 collaborative could be promising, and asked whether DOD could play a role in the diversity of the professoriate. Finally, he said, allocations to support systemic change and sustainability are important, so that projects can go forward irrespective of shifting state budgets and priorities.

San José State University

Dr. Erogbogbo centered his discussion on the importance of messaging about DOD opportunities. He said a main challenge is that most undergraduates do not know DOD. He urged capturing their interest to want to do DOD or related work. Faculty members also often think first of NSF or NIH to fund their research, and it is also important to invest in faculty so they pursue DOD funding. He agreed with previous panelists about challenges related to time and resources but urged finding ways "to pierce student interests." For example, a program at San José State during Black Engineer Week is a faculty-in-residence initiative. Engaging in other spaces also helps students envision their pathway. As a promising model, he pointed to a summer engineering program at SJSU.[9] He suggested a similar DOD initiative that is flexible with no barriers to entry. Pairing students with engineers also has impact, he concluded.

---

[9] For more information on programs of the San José Engineering Student Success Center, see https://www.sjsu.edu/essc/.

Alaska Native and Native Hawaiian Institutions

The final panel of this session brought in representatives from ANNHSI institutions: Helen Turner, Ph.D. (Chaminade University of Honolulu), Aaron Dotson, Ph.D. (University of Alaska Anchorage [UAA]), and Michele Yatchmeneff, Ph.D. (University of Alaska Anchorage).

Chaminade University of Honolulu

Dr. Turner noted that Chaminade is a Pacific institution that "is small but is punching above its weight." It has 1,200 students, is faith based, and is "matrix marginalized" in that students are poor, Indigenous, and isolated geographically. Chaminade fosters a sense of belonging and attainment and considers itself a "C1"—community first—institution. She stressed the value of being "between knowledges, Indigenous and western." Climate change, a nuclear legacy, and other issues affect the culture, health, equity issues, and environment of the Pacific.

Dr. Turner pointed to the geopolitical importance of the region, transitioning from an aid model, and the value of tapping into Pacific ways of knowing and doing. Over the past 15 years, Chaminade has built a portfolio around inclusion for students, meaningful research, workforce development aligned with regional needs, and capacity building. According to Dr. Turner, its total portfolio of NSF awards is about $43 million and funds a data science program, cyber infrastructure, and scholarships, among other efforts. Its NIH portfolio focuses on AI and health inequity, and it also receives U.S. Air Force funding, which she said has been transformative.

True partnerships have been a feature in the growth, Dr. Turner continued. Several are long term, and they are managed through a collective impact framework to create mutually shared agendas and document progress. An example is a successful data science program for Native Hawaiians, formerly incarcerated people, veterans, and others. She said it is important for agencies to understand Chaminade's journey, moving from being dismissed in 2007 (when they had never had a federal grant and no research capability) to the present. The transition was characterized by a conducive institutional environment, committed champions, relationships, extraordinarily committed faculty, alignment with regional and national priorities, and laser focus on outcomes and proof points. The growth began with sub-awards that showed the institution was a valued partner based on outcomes. More substantial awards have followed, which has strengthened Chaminade's agency over its own future while also advocating for other institutions in the Pacific region. She countered incorrect assumptions expressed by some reviewers about smaller institutions' capabilities. She noted DOD was an early believer in Chaminade, beginning with support from the Air Force in 2008. The credibility gained from that support was leveraged with other funders and other DOD programs and defense contractors.

Dr. Turner offered several recommendations to build research capacity for institutions like Chaminade: (1) a national systemized effort to mitigate personal and professional biases that contaminate review processes, restack review panels, and recognize the difference between excellence and elitism; (2) a national systemized effort to reintroduce/revalue non-R1 identities in science; (3) mandated trickledown, especially in single R1/R2 states, and a reward to R1 institutions for joint faculty appointments; (4) equity in funding mechanisms; (5) a nationally coordinated effort to assist small institutions and help them scale; (6) subsidized faculty workload models based on service to populations/regions/needs; (7) federally funded career development awards for resilient champions; and (8) mitigation against academic trafficking and commoditization, so that institutions and students are valued and not just used as a diversity checkbox.

University of Alaska Anchorage

Dr. Dotson highlighted research support at the University of Alaska Anchorage, including programs funded by DOD, the Department of Homeland Security (DHS), and other agencies. Dr. Yatchmeneff, an Alaska Native who is from an Aleutian community, described some of the region's global and military interactions. She added she is the only Alaska Native in the world with a Ph.D. in engineering education, and there are currently only three Alaska Natives with Ph.D.'s in engineering. She is serving as UAA's first Alaska Native Education and Outreach executive director, at the vice chancellor level.

UAA is not officially considered an MSI because that designation is based on percentage of a single population, Dr. Dotson explained.[10] How-

[10] Dr. Dotson noted UAA is not officially considered an MSI, which is based on the 2022 Department of Education's Eligibility Matrix. UAA is now officially considered an MSI, per the 2023 Eligibility Matrix. For information to compare the 2022 Matrix to the 2023 Matrix at the Department of Education's Office of Postsecondary Education, see https://www2.ed.gov/about/offices/list/ope/idues/eligibility.html. The Rutgers Center for Minority Serving Institutions maintains a directory of current, 2023 eligible MSIs, based on Department of Education data at https://cmsi.gse.rutgers.edu/msi-directory.

ever, 60 percent of local K–12 students are of diverse backgrounds, as are 50 percent of UAA students, 11 percent of whom are Indigenous.

DOD performs Arctic exercises out of Alaska, and DOD and DHS have strong presences in the state. Being a community partner is important because the military is important to the community. For example, UAA works with the Army Corps of Engineers on place-based research, such as a study to help the military understand the effects of its work on salmon. The DHS Arctic Domain Awareness Center and new DOD Ted Stevens Center for Arctic Security Studies also integrate with UAA academic programs. UAA stresses the nature of being inclusive, where students are provided places of community, culture, and refuge. Many faculty are transient and move to the state for the job, so they need to learn about living and working in Alaska. The Indigenous connection is intrinsic at UAA and extends beyond those with Indigenous backgrounds.

Dr. Yatchmeneff stressed that building relationships takes time. A connection to the land is often not included in a research plan, which misses a lot of helpful information, she said. As an example of a successful program, the Alaska Native Science and Engineering Program (ANSEP) began in 1995 with one student and now serves kindergarten to Ph.D. students on the UAA campus.[11] Students can move from grade 8 to a bachelor's degree in 5 years, with internships, research opportunities, and other experiences. She participated in "Alaska Grown PhD," through which she earned her Ph.D. and returned to UAA as faculty. She stressed the importance of involving precollege students in STEM, to include financial support.

As another application of the concept of Alaska Grown PhD, Dr. Dotson added that interns often become employees, and DOD has the opportunity to grow the employees of the future. The Alaska Native Success Initiative has been launched for students and faculty to help Alaska Native success across all University of Alaska campuses so that efforts do not just rely on a few individuals.[12]

REIMAGINING FACULTY WORKLOAD POLICIES

The next session of the town hall looked at faculty workloads in the context of building research capacity. In a consideration of building capacity

[11] For more information on ANSEP, see https://www.ansep.net.

[12] For more information on the Alaska Native Success Initiative, see https://www.alaska.edu/pres/aknativesuccess/.

at MSIs, invariably faculty engagement is brought up as the linchpin to growing the enterprise, Dr. Barton commented in introducing Mark Ginsberg, Ph.D. (George Mason University), and John Crockett, Ph.D. (San Diego State University [SDSU]). They described faculty workload models at their institutions, then engaged in discussion with Dr. Barton.

Two Models: George Mason University and San Diego State University

George Mason University is the largest R1 in Virginia, Dr. Ginsberg began, with 40,000 students and 2,000 educators as instructional research (IR), administrative and professional, and adjunct faculty. The IR faculty is composed of two categories—tenure track (2/2 teaching load,[13] expected to be research active) and term, also called contract or contingent. Term faculty sign a contract for 1 year and are later eligible for 3- or 5-year contracts. The teaching load varies, but it is usually 4/4, although some are engaged in research. Dr. Ginsberg stressed that the distinction between tenure-track and term faculty has to do with workload expectations, not esteem or respect. He said an institution needs a range of faculty who research, teach, and split their time between the two.

Dr. Crockett said San Diego State University is designated an HSI and AANAPISI (Asian American and Native American Pacific Islander–Serving Institution) and is the most research active of the 23 campuses in the CSU system at about $165–170 million per year. It is aiming to transition to R1 status. A separate, nonprofit organization manages grants and contracts. Dr. Crockett noted that an artifact of the 1960 Donahoe Higher Education Act is that SDSU offers graduate programs, but Ph.D.s must be delivered through another institution.[14] SDSU has recently prioritized the engagement of postdoctoral scholars and made a number of matching investments in extending postdocs on campus. Dr. Crockett said one advantage of the San Diego area is that when faculty transition away from teaching to research, a large pool of people to engage as contingent faculty is available.

Dr. Crockett noted the multiple time demands on SDSU faculty, including teaching, mentorship, training, and research involvement, adding that women and historically excluded faculty tend to spend more time on class preparation than majority faculty. He noted that faculty at SDSU

[13] In academic parlance, a 2/2 teaching load typically means two classes per semester, whereas a 4/4 is typically the highest, at four courses per semester.

[14] For more information, see https://oac.cdlib.org/view?docId=hb5b69n9fm&brand=oac4&doc.view=entire_text.

and other MSIs make an intentional choice to be "radically available" to students, but this adds to their workloads. He offered several ideas from the Division of Research and Innovation to lessen the faculty load, noting that students often seek faculty for navigational assistance and not just academic content. Moreover, students preferentially seek out women and underrepresented minority faculty to deal with these issues. For example, faculty can now refer students to other resources on campus that can better help them, such as for issues related to food or housing insecurity. Another strategy is to consider aspects of research that can be done by someone who does not have a Ph.D., such as editing, pre-submission review, and biosketches. His office also helps faculty engage in small groups to overcome isolation.

Dr. Crockett urged federal agencies to interrogate their review practices and biases related to applications from MSIs. He related that he has served on review panels where reviewers do not understand the context of these institutions and some context could enhance the quality of the review. At many MSIs, the PI does everything, including human resources, procurement, and other administrative and management tasks. Additional funding for postdocs or project managers could increase research activity. A more sophisticated treatment of teaming among institutions is necessary, he agreed, and noted that SDSU also receives token invitations to partner because of its MSI status. He called for interactions that are authentic and build capacity in real ways.

Discussion

In response to a question from Dr. Barton, Dr. Ginsberg explained that both term and tenure-track faculty have governance privileges and opportunities to serve in George Mason's Faculty Senate. Term faculty can serve in administrative positions, as department chairs, and in senior leadership. The university tries to link salaries to the market. Creating a fair way to create competitive wages and also retain faculty is an area of challenge, he acknowledged.

Dr. Crockett considered ways to incentivize faculty to engage in DOD research. SDSU was involved in a program with North Dakota State University that looked at MSI faculty attitudes toward research. The study found that it is useful to attend to the morale of scholars and allow their natural excellence to emerge. Rather than focus on the outcomes side and push for more productivity, he said it is more helpful to pare down extra tasks so faculty can do what they were trained to do. He said postdocs also are a great investment to underpin the growth of research to be sustainable. They bring in energy and skills, and part of the educational responsibility of the institution is to prepare them to succeed in the research enterprise. Postdocs at SDSU receive support in building community and professional development.

CULTURAL AND LEADERSHIP MODELS TO FACILITATE RESEARCH CAPACITY BUILDING

In the final session of the first day of the town hall, Abigail Newsome, Ph.D. (Mississippi Valley State University), moderated a session about institutional programs and policies that have been responsive to DOD needs and priorities. Speakers were Jagannathan Sankar, Ph.D. (North Carolina Agricultural and Technical State University [N.C. A&T]), and Twyla Baker, Ph.D. (Nueta Hidatsa Sahnish College [NHSC]).

North Carolina Agricultural and Technical State University

Dr. Sankar discussed building a research infrastructure over time at North Carolina Agricultural and Technical State University using federal, state, and industrial collaborations and partnerships in the area of advanced materials and processes as an example. The first funded research was in ceramics, supported by NASA, followed by programs funded by the NSF, U.S. Army, U.S. Navy, and other entities. An interconnective advanced materials facility was built. Its most important feature, he stressed, was to create an innovation ecosystem that crosses disciplines. N.C. A&T made history in 2008 by leading and winning an NSF Engineering Research Center, the first HBCU to do so. N.C. A&T also set up the first bioengineering program at an MSI and is now working with The Ohio State University and other institutions and industries on hybrid autonomous manufacturing.

Dr. Sankar stressed the importance of self-evaluation for success. This involves knowing the areas where N.C. A&T excels, competitive advantages, foundational strengths, and how to sustain and lead in the years to come. Partnerships are based on strengths, rather than trying to do everything. He recommended a team approach across discipline areas with metrics to track as part of a self-evaluation. He uses a quad chart approach to map all projects by analyzing their significance, progress, continuation plans, and project extension. Data are mined to understand where students go on to work after graduation. Communication is very important, including with K–12 students. He also commented on the need for visionary dreamers, mentoring the next generation, and a focus on character and leadership as part of a "one team, one dream" philosophy.

Dr. Sankar stressed the need to build capacity over time. "Once you have a successful start, the success comes easier in later stages and people want to join," he said. N.C. A&T is the largest HBCU in the nation and is working to become an R1. To succeed, everyone from president to chancellor to dean to faculty must work in a similar direction, he concluded.

Nueta Hidatsa Sahnish College

Like other TCUs, Nueta Hidatsa Sahnish College on the Fort Berthold Indian Reservation began by addressing social and economic issues of tribal members mostly through career and adult education, explained Dr. Baker. She noted that TCUs that are chartered by tribal nations have funding structures, opportunities, and capacities that reflect their different priorities. NHSC conducts community-based and mission-driven applied research, for example related to food sovereignty and air quality. It is important to help with student employment either on or off the reservation. She said she must convey to partners that the institution is small and rural and is often the only accessible higher education option for students. Remedial education is offered, and they also look for partnerships with larger institutions to expose students to bench or field research.

Dr. Baker noted that TCUs often face a visibility question when grouped with other MSIs. In her experience, if tribal nations are not explicitly mentioned in a funding opportunity, they will be left out. It is important that advocates talk about native people because they are less than 1 percent of the higher education population, she said. This has been referred to as the "native asterisk": that is, the numbers of Native American, Native Hawaiian, and Alaska Natives are so small in datasets that there is an asterisk rather than a percentage number. Despite the small numbers, she stressed, "We need to be having these conversations. Innovation and knowledge systems since time immemorial are stored with tribal people."

Context is crucial in terms of physical resources, access to technology and other resources, and populations. Many communities do not trust federal agencies unless robust conversation takes place to build relationships based on mutual respect and prioritization of the goals. As an example of mutual benefit, her tribal nation has been in the same place for 13,000 years with deep knowledge of soil, water, and food that could be useful to DOD.

The missions of TCUs are multifaceted with a strong cultural component folded in, Dr. Baker continued. They are centers of innovation and translation but also must maintain culture and language for the next generation. Partners have to take that mission seriously, she said. Dr. Baker said her institution has a process in place to be thoughtful about which opportunities to pursue. Echoing other presenters, she expressed frustration when people seeking a TCU partner to submit a proposal contact her and require a quick sign-off.

The main point is to build a level of trust to envision a pathway forward, Dr. Baker said. She noted some faculty and tribal members have gone on to larger institutions and have built relationships with government, industry, and other universities. She acknowledged the large investment made in her education so she could return to work at NHSC and find opportunities for others. She seeks commitments with external partners to set goals together, some of whom are tribal members. Those who are not tribal members need to understand Indian Country, she concluded.

Discussion

Discussing the notion of "check-boxing" when partners come in at the last minute, Dr. Baker described NHSC's process in which proposals go through an executive committee and administration committee and, in some cases, the board. Capacity is already limited by other projects going on, and soft funding dollars almost match the general fund with a lot of different projects. Team members have to be judicious with time. She also said she keeps strong tabs on the health and well-being of staff and faculty so that they do not burn out.

Dr. Sankar noted two main types of partnerships for N.C. A&T: internal across disciplines within the university and external. In his view, the strongest external partnerships are based on authentic relationships between faculty members and colleagues at other institutions, agencies, or industry.

REFERENCE

Congressional Research Service. 2022. *Federal Research and Development (R&D) Funding: FY2022*. CSR R468869. https://crsreports.congress.gov/product/pdf/R/R46869.

3

Town Hall I, Day 2: Capacity Development through Funding Portfolios, Infrastructure, and Federal Programs

Highlights from the Presentations

- Data on performance, outcomes, and other measures are needed to create and sustain strong research programs (Riddick).
- Leaders at universities that want to pursue DOD and other contracts should understand the need to change institutional culture and policies, for example, related to teaching loads and how professors can attain tenure (McCrary).
- The mission of DOD is to equip the warfighter. Within this goal, research is needed in multiple fields that MSIs can undertake and are already undertaking (Arnold).

This list is the rapporteurs' summary of points made by the individual speakers identified, and the statements have not been endorsed or verified by the National Academies of Sciences, Engineering, and Medicine. They are not intended to reflect a consensus among workshop participants.

The second day of the April 24–25 Town Hall focused on how several institutions have built diverse funding portfolios over time, as well as ideas on what constitutes a critical threshold for infrastructure investments. It ended with presentations on capacity-building programs supported by the Department of Energy (DOE) and the National Science Foundation (NSF).

DEVELOPING A DIVERSE FUNDING PORTFOLIO

Workshop chair Oscar Barton, Ph.D., P.E. (Morgan State University), moderated the first session to gleam the necessary components of a diverse funding portfolio at higher education institutions. Speakers included Kamal Khayat, Ph.D. (Missouri University of Science and Technology [Missouri S&T]), and Renata Rawlings-Goss, Ph.D. (Georgia Institute of Technology/South Big Data Innovation Hub).

Missouri University of Science and Technology

Dr. Khayat explained that Missouri S&T is a land-grant institution that is a part of the University of Missouri System. The goal is to transition from R2 to R1, although he noted the challenge because the dominance of science, technology, engineering, and mathematics (STEM) has meant little research and no doctoral students in non-STEM subjects. Programs in business, technical writing, and psychology are being planned to broaden into non-STEM areas. University leaders undertook strategic planning to identify areas of growth, invest in and pursue large proposals in these core areas of strength, and build capacity in emerging areas such as Bio-X (biomedical and environmental science) and sustainability.

Through the establishment of nine research centers, multidisciplinary and multi-institutional proposals can be developed, and about 80 percent of indirect funds are submitted through the centers. Most are in STEM, although he called attention to the Center for Science, Technology, and Society that combines humanities, social sciences, and technology. Another area for fostering growth is through new initiatives, such as the Midwest Alliance for Clean Hydrogen funded by the Department of Energy.[1]

Missouri S&T also has a large portfolio of awards with industry, according to Dr. Khayat. Forty-one percent of research awards in FY 2022 were with industry compared with 36 percent with the federal government. Over the past 5 years of about $155 million in total, about 29 percent has been with industry, which he noted is more than comparative schools and is considered an area of growth. He commented that while most of the grants are not very large, they represent repeat business because the companies return to Missouri S&T for use-inspired research. Missouri S&T also

[1] For more information on the Midwest Alliance for Clean Hydrogen, see https://machh2.com/.

participates in research consortia with industry to pursue federal grants, the largest of which is the Peaslee Steel Manufacturing Research Center.[2] Other research consortia involve aerospace technology, construction engineering and management, and other areas. The consortia can be leveraged to go after federal grants such as the Industry-University Cooperative Research Center funded by the National Science Foundation, he added. Dr. Khayat underlined the "virtuous cycle" of working with industry through consortia. "If you do a good job, it is repeat business for the consortia and for consortia members," he said. In addition, students like to work on real-life problems, and, in many cases, the research sponsors become their employers.

Funding from the Department of Defense (DOD), Department of Health and Human Services, DOE, and NSF has grown at the institution. Dr. Khayat noted a high success rate on DOD proposals, which he attributed to "establishing relationships at DOD, delivering on time and budget—all are important to build capacity for the researchers to continue to get contracts and grants." He noted the value of subscribing to consortia, including the Medical Technology Enterprise Consortium and National Armaments Consortium. Membership usually costs from $500 to $1,000 annually and provides opportunities for education, publication of white papers, conferences, and networking. This is especially helpful for early-career researchers, he pointed out.

According to Dr. Khayat, a point of inflection for Missouri S&T was a transformational gift of $311 million to fund the Kummer Institute. The mandate is to elevate Missouri S&T, broaden STEM outreach to young people, and drive economic development in the state. A $1 million fund for educational and research grants provides $50,000 grants to faculty to build teams to compete for large proposals. Also, research centers have been established to help industry prototype, de-risk, and train the workforce in artificial intelligence, advanced manufacturing, resource sustainability, and advanced and resilient infrastructure. Some of the funds are for capital investment, with the Missouri Protoplex as the first of four planned buildings. Another will be the Bio-X Center for life sciences, engineering, sustainability, and environment.

Explaining how industry connections developed, Dr. Khayat said faculty meet industry representatives at conferences and by serving on technical committees. Workshops are held for early-career faculty to have the

[2] For more information, see https://mse.mst.edu/steelmanufacturingresearchcenter/.

mindset of helping industry solve problems. Also, through the consortia, researchers can work on a problem that affects multiple companies that would not normally work together as competitors.

Georgia Institute of Technology/South Big Data Hub

Dr. Rawlings-Goss explained that Georgia Tech is unique in that research spans three parts: the university, primarily for basic research; Georgia Tech Research Institute (GTRI) as a separate contracting arm, primarily for DOD; and the Georgia Tech Foundation for philanthropic efforts. The sponsored research at the university and GTRI combined was above $1 billion in 2019.

GTRI is a nonprofit applied research arm with 2,500 employees, mostly engineers and scientists. Annually, it serves about 200 clients within DOD. GTRI started in the 1920s, when the state legislature created it as an engineering experiment station along the lines of agricultural experiment stations. Employees are mostly self-funded through the contracts they bring in; they are not faculty, although some students come to GTRI as interns. She echoed the comments by others about the need to establish relationships and build a reputation to get contracts. In 2019, GTRI received a $245 million contract from the U.S. Air Force for software and technology that will support hundreds of systems for 60 different aircraft. With large contracts like this in mind, she explained the history of GTRI to show the benefit of starting small, building a niche, and concentrating in particular areas.

On the university side, Dr. Rawlings-Goss said the faculty portfolio is organized in Interdisciplinary Research Institutes (IRIs), which she described as internal coalition points and an external face. She is involved in an IRI on data engineering and science that brings together data-centric work across Georgia Tech's schools, colleges, and departments. The institute connects faculty who then can go after larger, cross-cutting opportunities. She commented that the days of large awards going to a single principal investigator (PI) working alone are mostly gone. Building the consortia within the university is key.

Dr. Rawlings-Goss is also director of the South Big Data Innovation Hub, funded by NSF, which aims to build economic development and capacity across the region.[3] The hub comprises 1,300 partners, including

[3] For details of the South Big Data Innovation Hub, see https://southbigdatahub.org.

R1s, industry, and federal, state, and local government, to solve grand challenges the country faces. She stressed the hub can help transfer best practices and strengthen partnerships through seed grants and other support. Awards in service to other institutions, such as through seed grants, sometimes do not get much attention, but they build trust and benefit everyone, she stressed. She noted one partnership with Historically Black Colleges and Universities (HBCUs) through the Data Science Consortium.[4] Dr. Rawlings-Goss closed by reiterating the need to coalesce around areas of strength through centers and institutes, taking advantage of external partnerships, and supporting grassroots efforts.

Discussion

Considering the lessons learned in how to build the Data Science Consortium with HBCUs, Dr. Rawlings-Goss described how a seed grant was used. In the first year, she connected with all members, and a central finance team helped everyone with procurement. She added that administrative staffing is critical to start-up, because faculty are busy, but back-office activities and communications are often left out of traditional awards but are needed to build a consortium. Dr. Rawlings-Goss said a win-win attitude is essential to solve grand challenges as a country. As the founding director of the data hub, she has worked to establish the culture of collaboration. Georgia Tech is one member, and she had to talk to leadership about the benefits of being a trusted partner. The narrative she has taken with leadership and with staff, she shared, is that a win for a partner is a win for all. She noted that a consortium can offer deep levels of expertise unmatched by individual members.

ADDRESSING THE CRITICAL THRESHOLD FOR INFRASTRUCTURE INVESTMENTS

This panel extended the dialogue into the area of critical infrastructure investment. Moderated by Chad Womack, Ph.D. (United Negro College Fund [UNCF]), the panelists were Jaret Riddick, Ph.D. (Center for Security and Emerging Technology [CSET]), Victor McCrary, Ph.D. (University of the District of Columbia [UDC]), and Shannon Arnold, M.Eng., M.S. (GBL Systems Corporation). Topics included an investigation of critical

[4] For more information on the HBCU Data Science Consortium, see http://hbcu-dsc.org.

thresholds, funding opportunities for infrastructure development, and strategies for institutions and DOD to consider toward support for research infrastructure.

The Need for Metrics

Dr. Riddick explained CSET is a think tank based at Georgetown University that works at the intersection of national security and emerging technology to provide insight to policymakers. He came to CSET after 20 years at DOD and, as an HBCU graduate, is a strong supporter of leveraging HBCUs to serve the nation. Referring to the National Academies of Sciences, Engineering, and Medicine study on defense research capacity, he called attention to the recommendations about improving data collection at DOD to assess critical areas, including by HBCUs and other Minority-Serving Institutions (MSIs), and to develop metrics to track progress (NASEM, 2022, Recommendation 3). "When we think about this infrastructure conversation, it's easy for us to see what's lacking, but I want to have a forward-looking conversation where we talk about how to construct real measures based on data to build strategies so that infrastructure investments align with national security," Dr. Riddick said.

He pointed to Section 223 of the FY 2023 National Defense Authorization Act,[5] which calls for a pilot program, partly inspired by the National Academies report (NASEM, 2022) and by the HBCU RISE Act,[6] in which Congress mandated the secretary of defense to create a 10-year program to help MSIs and HBCUs move from R2 to R1. "So, there is great language and a charge, but to understand where we are going, we need formidable and formalized metrics," he said. Redefinition of the Carnegie Classification system in 2018 provided new opportunities, he continued. The number of R1s has doubled, and there is a broader perspective about what an R1 looks like. Quality comes in all shapes and sizes, and the funding profile of new R1s looks like the top HBCU R2s, he observed.

Publicly available data provide useful information, Dr. Riddick continued. For example, data of new-entrant R1s and the equipment they

---

[5] See https://www.congress.gov/bill/117th-congress/house-bill/7776/text.

[6] The HBCU RISE Act, designed to increase research capacity at HBCUs through a pilot project to fund equipment, instrumentation, and facilities, was incorporated into the National Defense Authorization Act and signed by President Biden on December 23, 2022. See https://new.nsf.gov/funding/opportunities/centers-research-excellence-science-technology-0.

purchased over the past few years can be tracked.[7] Similarly, data from the HBCU-MI (Minority Institutions) instrumentation program can show what is being purchased and understand trends. In his view, the critical areas identified in this program do not necessarily align with actual Office of the Under Secretary of Defense for Research and Engineering critical technology areas. "If we are trying to be sure that we are effective in developing research capacity, we want to be sure that we are aligning with the actual priorities of DOD," he stated. He noted that the Section 223 mandate is an opportunity to have the secretary of defense and DOD weigh in about critical technology areas so that HBCUs can ensure they are aligning with DOD priorities.

Historically Black Colleges and Universities as a National Security Asset

Dr. McCrary described his background as a Washington, DC native and part of a military family, graduate of Howard University, and leader with industry, government, and universities. He was involved in DOD through work at the Johns Hopkins University Applied Physics Laboratory, which is a University Affiliated Research Center (UARC). He focused on internal research and development and spent about $1 million with HBCUs. "I believed if we were looking for innovations for the country, we could not keep investing in the same lakes and ponds," he said. He is currently at the University of the District of Columbia, the land-grant institution of Washington, DC (Dr. McCrary also spoke at the May 22 Town Hall; see Chapter 4).

There were 11 R2 HBCUs at the time of the town hall, according to Dr. McCrary. Figures from 2020 show that DOD has increased expenditures in these institutions, but at a fraction of the resources going to R1s. To increase the amount, research administrative talent is needed, he said. Most institutions lack sufficient staff who have familiarity with grants, cooperative agreements, and contracts; research security and integrity considerations; and technology commercialization. As an opportunity, he called attention

---

[7] Dr. Riddick referred to the DOD's Defense University Research Instrumentation Program (DURIP), a funding mechanism for purchasing research instrumentation and equipment for high-quality defense-related research. In September 2019, the Institute for Defense Analyses conducted a review of publicly available data from the DURIP program. See https://www.ida.org/research-and-publications/publications/all/r/re/review-of-defense-university-research-instrumentation-program-durip.

to NSF's Growing Research Access for Nationally Transformative Equity and Diversity (GRANTED) program in which smaller institutions share this infrastructure (see presentation below). Another suggestion he made for attracting talent is the DARPA Innovation Fellowship Program.[8]

In August 2022, as one of the councils funded by the Universities Space Research Association, the HBCU Science and Technology Council was established.[9] The council comprises vice presidents from nine institutions (additional invitations have been extended) to align with NASA centers and DOD areas and to exchange best practices and experiences. Partnerships are important, and there are enough resources to go around. He lauded the recent UARC established at Howard University and noted that UDC has agreements with three other UARCs to support access to instrumentation, internships, research experiences, and other efforts.

Dr. McCrary stressed the importance of technology transfer. He noted that research conducted at Tuskegee University resulted in more than 300 inventions but only three patents (none filed on behalf of Tuskegee itself), so that the institution does not benefit from the research. By contrast, African American engineer and inventor Percy Julian, Ph.D., who applied for patents for his research and founded his own lab, understood commercialization. UDC held no patents when Dr. McCrary arrived 5 years ago, but now has 14 provisional patents and more are in process. He stressed a new university paradigm that encompasses both academic and entrepreneurial aspects. The value proposition to DOD is patents and commercialization, rather than traditional academic outputs like papers, he concluded.

Partnering in the Future Operational Environment

Mr. Arnold has subject-matter expertise in autonomy and artificial intelligence. Partnering with DOD means supporting the warfighter, which requires everything from outer space to under the sea, he stressed. "Your school is probably doing something relevant," he posited, listing software engineering, mechanical engineering logistics, medicine, materials, and other areas. "You are not outside the scope; it is a matter of partnering to bring that forward. The battleground is about putting technology into the warfighter's hands."

---

[8] For more information, see https://www.darpa.mil/work-with-us/darpa-innovation-fellowship.

[9] For more information, see https://newsroom.usra.edu/new-hbcu-science-and-technology-council-established-at-universities-space-research-association/.

DOD staff can assist institutions and faculty in identifying opportunities, he said, such as the director and staff of the HBCU/MI Program in the Office of the Under Secretary of Defense. He urged getting involved with UARCs to have access to larger amounts of funding. He took note of the UARC at Howard and the advocacy role of many people to make it happen. In addition to the support to the HBCU, Mr. Arnold pointed to workforce issues. In 2030, a large percentage of DOD will be at retirement age and students at HBCUs can provide the talent as a win-win for the country and universities.

Stressing the range of services and technologies needed by DOD, he urged HBCUs and other MSIs to "get your foot in the door." Institutions without the infrastructure can start with the DOD Mentor-Protégé Program, in which large companies work with universities to help serve DOD.[10] He also suggested contacts with R1s and with UARCs to get training and leverage infrastructure. Howard is now setting up its infrastructure, getting clearances, and other needs to establish its UARC. "The money is out there once relationships are built," he said. The language in the National Defense Authorization Acts shows technical areas that are important to DOD, he pointed out.[11] He also noted that schools located near military bases and testing ranges, many of which are in the South, can work with their nearby DOD installations.

Discussion

Dr. Womack noted HBCUs' strong base of teaching and posed whether the requirements for R&D, especially commercialization, are asking faculty to do too much. "Would we be better positioned if we look at teaching as a core premise and lift that up as an essential component, but also build out space for researchers to be on campus or affiliated who are focused on research?" he queried. Dr. McCrary concurred with the pressure of teaching loads. The issue requires conversations at the top with boards of trustees. He said it is important for HBCUs and other MSIs not to give up their legacy as teachers, but to go after opportunities at DOD and other agencies through multiple pathways. It is about culture change, he suggested. With contracts, faculty can be hired on research lines.

---

[10] For more information, see https://business.defense.gov/Programs/Mentor-Protege-Program/.

[11] For more information, see https://www.congress.gov/bill/118th-congress/house-bill/2670/text.

He cautioned institutions not to make too many requests for no-cost extensions when money cannot be spent because of teaching loads. "We have to start the conversations with the provosts, deans, and the boards to understand how the landscape has changed," he said. "If they want to bring in these new opportunities, they cannot operate with faculty hamstrung with teaching or policies that are outdated." For example, many faculty on DOD work cannot publish, but professors are penalized for lack of publications when they go up for tenure. Dr. Barton said he supported models of collaboration and contract building but noted that a university is set up toward knowledge generation. "I think it is scary for us to say that we want to have an institution that completely disaggregates the ability for our faculty members to engage in knowledge generation because of resource generation," he cautioned.

Dr. Riddick commented that when he was involved in internal collaborations at DOD, it created a problem when institutions received grants but were slow in spending the money. "People are less willing to accept that universities have slow burn rates," he said. He also noted that emerging technologies create an "open canvas." In many cases, experts have not yet been identified as "the only show in town," which provides opportunities for many institutions to be at the table at ground zero. Related to the missions of universities if they are pursuing research opportunities, he said, "I come back to data." Using the University of Texas at El Paso (UTEP) as an example, he noted UTEP's mission is around first-generation Americans; furthermore, "They did not lose the mission, they even doubled down on it as they became an R1." He said in his role at CSET, he plans to make data available, help people understand those data, and build models based on the data.

Dr. McCrary stressed the need for HBCUs to be at the table. Senior leaders need to participate in relevant forums and boards. It is important to engage program officers to learn their expectations. Presidents and board members must understand that the game has changed, doors are open, and "this is the time to band together." Dr. Womack said UNCF and the Thurgood Marshall Center put together, with Google Research, an Applied Research Institute (see Chapter 5). An outgrowth of engagement with 12 university presidents, he suggested it can serve as a model for other cross-institutional partnerships. However, he also recognized the complexities across HBCUs and other institutions, with both public and private structures and with different pressures, mandates, assets, and resources.

Dr. Barton said that Carnegie Center representatives came to Morgan State University during a strategic planning effort to discuss how to attain R1 status. Dr. McCrary noted that UDC had not been including its law school in its degrees awarded in its IPEDS (Integrated Postsecondary Education Data System) data. The importance of a focused person to collect data under the vice president of research was recognized. In looking to attain R1 status, Dr. Riddick noted, "In the data, you will find complex interdependencies that can build a strategy that is nonintuitive." Modeling and metrics are important not just to reach but also to sustain a Carnegie designation.

Dr. Barton said for many on the pathway, it is important to build infrastructure to sustain operations. He suggested institutions talk with Carnegie representatives. Another participant commented on getting aging and failing infrastructure up to par. Everyone talks about new buildings while others are falling down, he commented. DOD cannot pay for this, but it was pointed out that a "DOD dollar" can be leveraged to get other resources in the long term. Dr. McCrary urged institutions to think big. "Sometimes we play checkers instead of chess. Who sits on the board of regents? Who appoints them?" he said. It is important that the boards of MSIs reflect current and future leaders, including those who can tap into resources for the institution with state legislators and other decision-makers. Mr. Arnold said it is important to leverage all options and connections to make the best case for an institution and how growing it benefits the community.

FEDERAL CAPACITY-BUILDING PROGRAMS

Several research capacity-building programs sponsored by federal agencies were mentioned by presenters during the town halls. A session moderated by Keith McGee, Ph.D. (Alcorn State University), brought in representatives from two agencies: Natalia Melcer (Department of Energy) and Dina Stroud, Ph.D. (National Science Foundation).

U.S. Department of Energy Office of Science

Ms. Melcer spoke about two new cross-cutting initiatives coordinated by the Office of Science at the Department of Energy: Reaching a New Energy Sciences Workforce (RENEW) and Funding for Accelerated, Inclusive Research (FAIR).[12] They are part of a larger effort to achieve diversity, equity, and inclusion at DOE and in DOE-supported work, she said.

FAIR and RENEW began with 16 listening sessions, including with people from MSIs, community colleges, and underrepresented communities, to understand barriers to participation in DOE. She reported the most frequent comments were about systemic barriers, lack of awareness of opportunities, implicit bias, unclear solicitation processes, inequitable access to equipment, recruitment, and mentoring. This input is being used to inform not only FAIR and RENEW but also other ongoing DOE efforts. Goals include to (1) support diverse participation and a sense of belonging for all project personnel; (2) avoid tokenism and require substantive roles for all partner institutions; (3) address structural and financial barriers to participation for MSIs; (4) address concerns of bias in peer review of MSIs; (4) expand outreach and engagement to attract broad interest and foster partnerships; (5) invest in long-term and sustainable research and training efforts; and (6) evaluate efforts for progress toward building institutional capacity and retaining underrepresented individuals in Office of Science research areas in the long term.

Overall changes in business practices include inserting explicit language in all funding solicitations to encourage applicants from underrepresented institutions to apply, targeted advertisements, and webinars for faculty and administrators. Program Policy Factors, which are part of the awards, announce the intent to prioritize proposals from underrepresented institutions, first-time applicants, and/or institutions not previously funded by the Office of Science. There is also an emphasis on increasing reviewer diversity.

RENEW, which began in December 2022, has a student focus.[13] Solicitations were issued from each DOE research office, with common principles that include outreach and focus on students from underrepresented institutions conducting research at DOE labs and directly addressing barriers raised by stakeholders. Proposals are required to include a plan to address diverse participation and a sense of belonging, and review criteria were developed to evaluate the quality and efficacy of the plan. To avoid tokenism, the proposals have to demonstrate substantive roles for underrepresented institutions, again with specific review subcriteria, she

---

[12] For information on RENEW, see https://science.osti.gov/Initiatives/RENEW. For information on FAIR, see https://science.osti.gov/Initiatives/FAIR.

[13] For more information on RENEW, see https://science.osti.gov/Initiatives/RENEW.

said. Structural and financial barriers are addressed with language explaining allowable costs related to teaching staff, administrative support, instrumentation, student stipends, and other costs. To address bias in peer review, reviewers from underrepresented institutions were recruited and an orientation was held for all reviewers on implicit bias awareness and mitigation strategies. Ms. Melcer noted that some opportunities support planning and seed grants to develop future proposals. In addition, the Workforce Development for Teachers and Students (WDTS) program is developing new pathways for students and faculty from non-R1 MSIs, community colleges, and underrepresented groups to promote equitable access to STEM training opportunities, build science identity, and cultivate a sense of belonging. She also highlighted pathway summer school programs for high school and early undergraduate students at national labs, as well as a Visiting Faculty program for faculty to collaborate with DOE labs to do research or develop curricula. WDTS will also lead the evaluation and assessment of RENEW to understand what is working and adjust as needed.

Ms. Melcer characterized FAIR as a companion piece to RENEW in that it is designed to build research programs, mostly at non-R1 MSIs and emerging research institutions (ERIs) as defined in the CHIPS + Science Act.[14,15] FAIR supports mutually beneficial relationships between these institutions and a national lab, Office of Science user facility, or R1 MSI. Support is provided to a PI or research team to perform basic research and is designed to complement the student-focused traineeships supported by RENEW. She pointed out that equipment and infrastructure investments are allowable costs.

"In sum, both of these programs aim to increase the diversity of individuals and institutions participating in Office of Science research and to build relationships with institutions historically underrepresented in the Office of Science research portfolio," Ms. Melcer concluded. She noted that RENEW made its first awards in December 2022, and FAIR, with its focus on faculty research, will be awarded in the coming months.

[14] For more information on CHIPS + Science Act, see https://www.congress.gov/bill/117th-congress/house-bill/4346.

[15] For more information on FAIR, see https://science.osti.gov/Initiatives/FAIR. ERIs are institutions of higher education with an established undergraduate or graduate program that has less than $50 million in federal research expenditures.

National Science Foundation GRANTED Program

Dr. Stroud discussed NSF's GRANTED program, but she also called attention to NSF's HBCU Excellence in Research (HBCU-EiR) as another resource to explore.[16]

She likened the Office of the Director at NSF as equivalent to a university's leadership. The Office of Integrative Activities is within the Office of the Director and is a central place for broadening participation across NSF. Programs in addition to GRANTED and HBCU-EiR include the Established Program to Stimulate Competitive Research, or EPSCoR; Major Research Instrumentation, or MRI; and Science and Technology Centers, or STC. According to Dr. Stroud, NSF funds about 25 percent of federally funded basic research, and MSIs received about 15 percent of proposals evaluated and awarded (see Figure 3-1). Overall, the number of institutions submitting and receiving awards has decreased, which is a source of concern, she said.

An agency priority goal is to increase participation from underrepresented investigators and institutions by 10 percent over the 2020 baseline by the end of 2023. All eight NSF directorates have programs to reach this goal. However, as Dr. Stroud pointed out from the GRANTED program language, "A strong enterprise relies on more than funding for the research itself." The research enterprise is composed of researchers (investigators, teams, and trainees), staff and administration, and the institutions and organizations where they work. GRANTED is designed to strengthen capacity to apply for and manage external funding from both within and outside NSF. Partnerships, compliance, security, analytics, and commercialization are among the underpinnings that are often unseen but important to success, she noted.

All these aspects are addressed in what Dr. Stroud described as the GRANTED Wheel, which has three central elements: (1) enhancing practices and processes, (2) developing and strengthening human capital, and (3) translating effective practices into organizational contexts through professional societies and organizations.

Dr. Stroud encouraged institutions to develop strategies that could work to "raise all boats" for nationally transformative models of all sizes. "We have operated too long on the belief that all institutions are functioning from a similar space of resources support infrastructure, when they are

[16] For information on HBCU-EiR opportunities, go to https://new.nsf.gov/funding/opportunities/historically-black-colleges-universities-2.

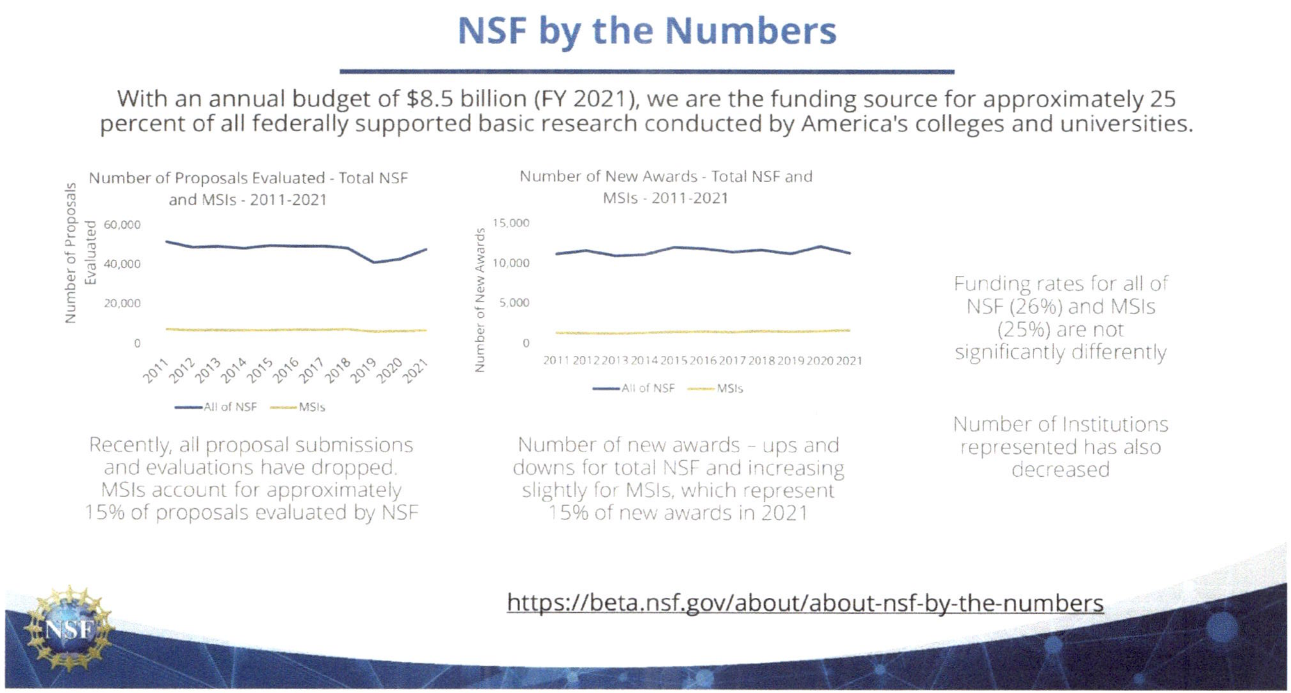

FIGURE 3-1 NSF proposal and award rates, 2011–2021.
SOURCE: Dina Stroud, Town Hall Presentation, April 25, 2023.

not," she said. She urged participants to learn more about GRANTED and to reach out to her and others at NSF.[17]

Discussion

Dr. McGee commented that the programs at both agencies show a thoughtful, deliberative look at the communities that are generally underserved and asked how the programs came about. Dr. Stroud explained a review of data about who is represented in the NSF portfolio showed no shift over time. She added that the Office of Integrative Activities director, Alicia Knoedler, had been a vice president of research at an institution and provided experience and observations from her perspective. Diving into the data, reflecting on it, and being intentional about acting can create change, she said. Dr. McGee commented that institutions sometimes take a micro look at data, but aggregated data could be useful. Ms. Melcer responded that DOE wanted to broaden participation across programs and to expose non-R1s to DOE opportunities. The hope is they will move into general research programs. Reviewer pools have been broadened, reaching people to serve on panels who may not be aware of the opportunities.

Dr. Barton commented that NSF and DOE awards represent a gold standard, and that, even when applicants are not successful, reviewer feedback is valuable for subsequent engagement. Dr. Stroud said NSF training materials stress that a review is not just a fund/do not fund decision but should provide constructive feedback to applicants. Ms. Melcer said that in working on new applicant tools it was important to provide more information about the review process, especially for those with less experience. In some cases, her office receives questions from faculty that a more robust university office of sponsored research could have helped with. The Office of Science is setting up webinars and more general outreach at the start of the fiscal year to explain opportunities. Dr. Stroud commented that to meet the expectation that institutions transfer to core research grants, resources are needed to make these transitions. Dr. Wolcott welcomed the programs and expressed the hope that they remain in place for an extended period of time. Ms. Melcer and Dr. Stroud said this is the intention at both agencies. "The drive is there, and it is growing, not shrinking," Dr. Stroud said.

---

[17] For more information about NSF 23-221Y (GRANTED), see https://new.nsf.gov/funding/opportunities/growing-research-access-nationally-transformative-0.

CONCLUDING REMARKS AFTER THE FIRST TOWN HALL

In the final session of the first town hall, workshop planning committee members shared some of their takeaways.

Dr. Barton reflected that the panels gave a sense that there is a long way to go, but opportunities can create a pathway going forward. As several presenters said, it is essential to advance the realization that faculty cannot do it all. A supportive and parallel structure is needed to enhance the research enterprise, he commented. For Tribal Colleges and Universities, HBCUs, Hispanic-Serving Institutions, and Alaska Native and Native Hawaiian–Serving Institutions, identity is important; it must be preserved in all engagements and can add value to the funders. Human capacity building is very important. Seeded throughout the presentations, he reflected, is the need to build frameworks over time. Institutions will have their own research initiatives, but they need to align with DOD research and technology initiatives to write credible proposals for DOD funding. Dr. Barton urged collecting data and making data-driven decisions to impact efforts, capitalizing on both well-established and innovative programs, and leveraging partnerships and consortia.

Dr. Wolcott urged messaging by agencies to communicate to institutions that they can participate in various opportunities. Faculty, who are busy with multiple responsibilities, may not realize that they are doing work that DOD needs. Conversely, DOD may not know about faculty who are undertaking research of value to its mission.

Dr. McGee commented that it is important to recognize that many professors at MSIs want to do research in support of teaching. Even if they are not at an R1 or R2 institution, they are looking for opportunities for their students so that they gain a solid foundation to go on to conduct cutting-edge research.

Dr. Newsome said it is important to keep the mission of the institutions in mind and balance innovation and cutting-edge research for the next generation, as well as increase the critical mind power of people who can look forward.

REFERENCE

NASEM (National Academies of Sciences, Engineering, and Medicine). 2022. *Defense Research Capacity at Historically Black Colleges and Universities and Other Minority Institutions: Transitioning from Good Intentions to Measurable Outcomes.* Washington, DC: The National Academies Press.

4

Town Hall II, Day 1: True Partnerships through the Research Ecosystem and Equitable and Synergistic Partnerships

Highlights from the Presentations

- It is critical for institutions to be at the table to understand research trends and opportunities, promote defense-industry research initiatives internally and externally, following the philosophy that there are "no permanent enemies or friends, just permanent interests" (McCrary).
- Co-location of industry–university facilities benefits the company and the university, with the proximity leading to greater collaboration and involvement (Devasia).
- BioMADE and other nonprofits offer a way to bring together multiple stakeholders to create a strong research ecosystem (Tubon).
- SBIR and STTR funding can be used to work with HBCUs and MSIs on emerging technology (Adolphe).
- An aspect of equity is to ensure that students receive adequate compensation for internships; otherwise, those who need to earn money are excluded from these opportunities (Deckard).

This list is the rapporteurs' summary of points made by the individual speakers identified, and the statements have not been endorsed or verified by the National Academies of Sciences, Engineering, and Medicine. They are not intended to reflect a consensus among workshop participants.

At the start of the second town hall, held in Albuquerque, New Mexico, on May 22 and 23, 2023, committee chair Dr. Oscar Barton, Jr., Ph.D., P.E. (Morgan State University), welcomed participants. He reviewed the agenda for the second town hall with its theme of building true partnerships between Minority-Serving Institutions (MSIs) and the Department of Defense (DOD) and other agencies, institutions of higher education, industry, and other stakeholders. The focus of the second town hall centered on the systems and components necessary to develop equitable partnerships with industry, non-minority institutions, and federal agencies with Minority Institutions (MIs) and the development of sustainable collaborations among MIs.

IGNITING THE DEFENSE RESEARCH ECOSYSTEM

In the first session, moderator Melvin Greer, Ph.D. (Intel Corporation), asked panelists to provide an overview about the stakeholders they consider relevant to a high-functioning research environment. The session spotlighted partnerships that have led to productive activities in research and development (R&D) and the matriculation of students into careers within the defense R&D environment. Participants were Victor McCrary, Ph.D. (University of the District of Columbia [UDC]), Santosh Devasia, Ph.D. (University of Washington), and Thomas Tubon, Ph.D. (BioMADE). Dr. Greer noted it is important to understand how institutions develop an ecosystem in order to support students in their defense or other science, technology, engineering, and mathematics (STEM) careers.

Three Examples of Research and Development Partnerhsips

University of the District of Columbia

Dr. McCrary noted that his work at UDC intersects with his role as vice chair of the National Science Board through a focus on research experiences for students and faculty to develop talent. As noted in Chapter 3, UDC is on track to become an R2 institution by 2024. Building the defense research ecosystem at UDC has involved buy-in from top leadership, with the Office of University Research as the nexus point. He stressed the importance of "being in the room" to understand trends and opportunities and to ensure equal partnerships, promoting defense-industry research initiatives internally and externally, and following the philosophy that there are "no permanent enemies or friends, just permanent interests."

UDC has partnerships with three University Affiliated Research Centers (UARCs) (at Pennsylvania State University; University of Maryland, College Park; and Johns Hopkins University); is developing activities with the U.S. Navy, National Security Agency, and U.S. Army; and is part of the new Historically Black Colleges and Universities (HBCU) Science and Technology (S&T) Council (see Chapter 3).

Dr. McCrary offered several reasons why a research ecosystem may not succeed, including if the vice president for research lacks strategic authority to make and close deals; there is a lack of cultural competency; the pay-off versus time and effort does not materialize; expectations are not balanced; and transactional, versus transformational, relationships are formed. MSIs offer the ability to produce a skilled workforce that can receive security clearances, which are needed in many opportunities in the CHIPS + Science Act and in DOD work.[1] He noted several provisions of the CHIPS + Science Act of particular interest for HBCUs and MSIs: University Technology Centers; increased funding for community colleges; authorization of increased funding for the Technology, Innovation, and Partnerships (TIP) Directorate at the National Science Foundation (NSF) (see Chapter 5 for more detail); and targeting of emerging research institutions to increase research capacity. In terms of workforce, Dr. McCrary stressed that talent is needed from the "missing millions," particularly Latin and Black talent. Growth of a skilled technical workforce is critical. HBCUs are ready for defense investment in terms of talent and innovation, he emphasized.

Boeing Advanced Research Center at the University of Washington

Dr. Devasia explained that the Boeing Advanced Research Center (BARC) at the University of Washington was put together over a period of 10 years and is an example of how to build and maintain a relationship with industry. The idea emerged from a university strategic planning effort to focus on the unique strengths of the region, including its port and industrial base, with Boeing, Microsoft, Amazon, and other companies headquartered in the Seattle region. The question was how to leverage this high-tech industrial base.

Dr. Devasia commented that industry's traditional funding model is to provide money, maybe receive some intellectual property (IP), and provide

---

[1] For more information, see https://www.congress.gov/bill/117th-congress/house-bill/4346.

internships or other opportunities for students. In contrast, BARC is a co-located effort dedicated to the transformation of manufacturing through development of advanced robotics, data analytics, and tools safety. BARC provides Boeing access and formation of relationships with undergraduate and graduate students. High-impact collaborative research projects are mentored by Boeing engineers. Students go on-site to Boeing, and Boeing engineers also come to campus. According to Dr. Devasia, universities tend to focus on fundamental work with low technology readiness levels, but this applied research has had incredible impact because students learn by doing and they are highly engaged.

It took a few years to figure out how the university and Boeing could best work together, Dr. Devasia explained. Issues included who owns the IP, alignment of research needs, and different funding cycles (fiscal year versus university calendar). Solutions that worked include prepackaged IP with a fixed cost; alignment by leveraging Boeing funding with other sources; and having a mix of students (bachelor's, master's, doctorate) on each project to facilitate academy and industry needs. Professional master's program students have also worked well in this setting.

BioMADE

Dr. Tubon agreed with the challenges identified by previous presenters, and noted they often surface with little movement to be addressed. He suggested that nonprofits and similar entities could bring different stakeholders together. BioMADE was launched in 2021 as a design and manufacturing ecosystem to bring together industry and educational institutions involved in bioindustrial manufacturing. Different sectors come together for an all-hands approach to promote applied research and commercialization. BioMADE embraces a multifaceted approach to realize the value that each stakeholder brings and overcome the breaks in the chain to provide additional support. He noted BioMADE rests on three pillars: technology and innovation; education and workforce development (his area of focus); and social dimensions (safety, security, sustainability, and social responsibility).

Discussion

Dr. Greer described an ecosystem as a complex network of interconnected pieces that operate seamlessly, and he asked participants to apply this concept to research. Dr. McCrary pointed to the need for a strategy to develop a research ecosystem, for example, to impact the community and to align with the National Science Board 2030 strategy for global leadership. This alignment leads to steps to pursue, he said. For example, UDC has great research labs but never had patents, so he brought in consultants to develop commercialization capacity. It is important to update policies and procedures and to engage in constant dialogue. Universities must recognize faculty culture but also the culture of funders related to timelines and other needs.

Dr. Greer agreed that stakeholders have different views about value, timelines, and measurements. As an example of different groups working together, Dr. Devasia suggested the ARM (Advanced Robotics for Manufacturing) Institute, which is funded by the secretary of defense and is part of the Manufacturing USA network.[2] Dr. Tubon concurred that the ARM Institute and other manufacturing institutes are a great model to bring stakeholders together. Funded projects can support research, education, and other programs for systems-level change. As an example, BioMADE supports about 50 projects, such as one in the Appalachian Highlands to support rural communities to engage in technology. As other examples, Dr. McCrary offered the Regional Innovation Hubs in the NSF TIP Directorate, as well as its Advanced Technological Education programs.

Dr. Greer echoed that building an ecosystem requires a central person who is primarily responsible to understand national priorities and align mechanisms with the desired end state. Dr. Tubon commented that it is important to interpret ecosystems as dynamic to move forward. He noted that many workforce development programs are pushing the envelope. Alone, they have done a great job, but in collaboration with others and breaking down silos, much more can be achieved, he posited.

Dr. Greer asked about situations where an ecosystem fails to ignite. Dr. Devasia suggested that the reason often comes down to different cultures and viewpoints. "It is a work in progress," he suggested, and noted that ecosystems may take many years of discussions and start with small steps before larger-scale interactions. Dr. McCrary commented that another impact when an ecosystem fails to ignite is a lack of trust that may cross over to other opportunities. Potential partners may become more risk-averse, which sets the ecosystem back and harms the community at large. The question to keep in mind is whether a particular model is the right fit for you and your system, and it may be a combination of several models, noted Dr. Tubon.

---

[2] For more information on the ARM Institute, see https://arminstitute.org/.

When asked by Dr. Greer for one factor that institutions must do to create and sustain ecosystems, Dr. Devasia underscored leadership and the willingness to see the long term. Dr. Tubon urged participation with manufacturing institutes around the country. Dr. McCrary pointed to working with local chambers of commerce and other leaders to understand on-the-ground realities.

ARTICULATING THE VALUE PROPOSITION FOR EQUITABLE PARTNERSHIPS

Transitioning from the first panel, Dr. Barton drew on Dr. McCrary's comment about the importance of "being at the table." That said, he continued, "We may be at the table, but is that enough for strong partnerships and alliances?" Three panelists shared what equitable partnerships could look like: Eric Adolphe, Esq. (Forward Edge-AI, Inc.), Christina Deckard (Office of the Under Secretary of Defense, Biotechnology), and Robert St. Amant, Ph.D. (DEVCOM Army Research Laboratory).

Context

The presenters briefly introduced their work to explain their perspectives about partnerships. Forward Edge-AI is an African American–owned small business that focuses on artificial intelligence (AI) solutions for defense, national security, and public safety, Mr. Adolphe explained. Since its inception, the company has worked with seven HBCUs and MSIs on Small Business Innovation Research (SBIR) and Small Business Technology Transfer Research (STTR) awards for DOD and NSF. Forward Edge-AI works with HBCUs and MSIs to build research capacity by leveraging these SBIRs and STTRs, and they fielded the first minority-owned, deep tech HBCU team that has been awarded Phase 1, 2, and 3 SBIRs. In undertaking these engagements, Mr. Adolphe commented, an important thing that comes out is that faculty, especially at HBCUs, consider themselves working at teaching institutions devoted to instruction, so there can be some tension between that vision and the DOD and private-sector missions. Students may not understand how they play into the mission of the nation or see the fruits of their labor, and he suggested finding ways to foster their sense of value in going from lab to market.

After a career as a Navy civilian scientist, Ms. Deckard now provides contract support to the Office of the Under Secretary of Defense for

Research and Engineering in Biotechnology, as the Biotechnology Office Education and Workforce Development lead. Biotech is a critical technology, and education and workforce are key, she said. She clarified that her ideas are her own and not representing DOD or her contractor, but hoped the town hall conversations can lead to better engagement.

Dr. St. Amant spent 20 years in the computer science department at North Carolina State University before joining the Army Research Lab. He was first involved in intramural research, but moved to manage extramural research last year. He is in charge of the Knowledge Systems Program and works with the Institute for Creative Technologies (ICT), which is a UARC located at the University of Southern California (USC).

Building on Partnerships

Ms. Deckard reminded the group that DOD has a number of programs that aim to form partnerships, such as the HBCU Centers of Excellence. While they are important ways for DOD to work with HBCUs, she acknowledged there is usually limited partnering. She commented that there are many other opportunities at NSF, DOD, and other agencies that she has less familiarity with even after a long career with DOD, which she noted shows the need to shed more light on them. For example, she called attention to NSF's Industry-University Cooperative Research Centers as an interesting model to provide value to all stakeholders (see Figure 4-1). Industry has access to talent, research results, and IP, as well as leveraged research dollars. Universities gain funding, industry insights, and student placements. Government gains leveraged research dollars, networks, and training. In any successful partnership, she stressed, each stakeholder must gain value, and it is more than just "checking a box."

Dr. Barton highlighted the theme of value to each partner. Mr. Adolphe noted the value added for his company is a straight line: "We are conducting research, developing products and IP, sharing that IP with the HBCUs and MSIs involved, and we want to monetize it." As a best practice, he pointed to a cooperative research agreement that required bringing in an HBCU partner. After initial research under the agreement, they applied for SBIRs, and have three MSIs developing new technology for DOD and for the commercial market. He noted that HBCU students are included in the IP and are named in the patent. Focusing on benefits to students, Mr. Adolphe noted that many students would never have considered the

FIGURE 4-1 Industry-University Cooperative Research Centers model.
SOURCE: Christina Deckard, Town Hall Presentation, May 22, 2023, from NSF (http://iucrc.nsf.gov).

concept of IP as a path to economic success. Projecting out, students who become entrepreneurs and business owners can benefit their alma maters, Dr. Barton commented, while Mr. Adolphe added that universities can also gain residual income from the IP.

Dr. St. Amant looked at the value added for the Army through the ICT UARC. The Army wanted an institute to improve simulation and saw the concentration of expertise and interest in filming and gaming in Southern California. For ICT and USC, the support raises visibility to DOD and other government agencies, which is good for the university, researchers, and students.

Ms. Deckard urged finding ways to compile good ideas and programs as best practices and articulate what the benefits are. "How can we message what the right thing is and make it so universities want to participate? It's important to pull this together and have the story," she said.

In interacting with emerging technology, Mr. Adolphe said his company looks at topics of interest posted by DOD and others. He reaches out to partners in HBCUs and MSIs to see who has expertise in the topics to pursue opportunities. He noted this works efficiently because his company has already established trust with its partners. Looking at disruptive technologies, Dr. St. Amant opined that academic researchers have more freedom to pursue ideas that industry may not be able to solve and government may not be agile enough to undertake. Ms. Deckard said that DOD is looking at a wide range of biotechnology applications, with many areas of exploration such as fuels and fabrics. She suggested finding ways to get the word out how HBCUs and MSIs can participate.

Dr. Barton asked about equitable partnerships across university types with changing student demographics. Mr. Adolphe responded that Forward Edge-AI tries to reflect the communities where they are, and students working on Forward Edge-AI projects reflect the demographics of their communities. Dr. St. Amant noted the benefit when students go on to work for industry or the government. He recalled the usefulness of an Industrial Advisory Council set up at North Carolina State University, many members of which were alumni. They understood the needs of both industry and the university and provided feedback in both directions. Ms. Deckard underscored the need for respecting the demographic composition of each region of the country. Regional hubs can provide a way to instill diversity as the norm in terms of racial, ethnic, and socioeconomic composition, as well as diversity of thought.

Dr. Barton commented that NSF proposals are structured to address intellectual merit and broader impacts, and he asked if equitable partnerships could be considered as part of a broader impact in this context. Mr. Adolphe commented that when he has served as an NSF peer reviewer, he looks for how broader impacts will move the needle in the specific S&T area being proposed, but not all applicants pay attention to this. He added when he submits a proposal to NSF, he addresses broader impacts that are measurable and hopes competitors are doing the same. Dr. St. Amant underscored the need for diversity in development teams to avoid bias, for example, in AI applications. Ms. Deckard urged being intentional about what is meant by broader impact. "Let's be clear about the purpose of a partnership," she said. An outcome could be that R1s and R2s are mentoring universities and colleges so that they are prepared to take the lead in the future, she suggested. Mr. Adolphe strongly agreed with the need for capacity building in partnerships, not just transactional agreements to meet a proposal requirement.

Returning to the issue of outcomes and deliverables, Mr. Adolphe commented that he held four jobs as an undergraduate, including security guard, loan processor, package loader, and engineering intern at the Federal Aviation Administration. This latter, which was a true passion and exposed him to the mission of public safety, paid the least. "As far as equity is concerned, the outcome is to encourage students to go into STEM public service, but there needs to be an alignment about why it is important," he said. Ms. Deckard praised the value of internships, but noted many are unpaid or barely paid. A student who must earn money cannot access them, which is where equity comes in.

Dr. Barton commented that in addition to internships, distributed experiences across a student's pathway can build careers. Mr. Adolphe said relationships should be deep and enduring. He suggested a role for "sherpas": people with domain and technical expertise, perhaps retired professionals, who can serve as navigators for institutions to build their research capacity. Institutions that have been doing this work for decades have a built-in advantage, he commented, and it will take a while for others to catch up. Ms. Deckard suggested mentorship at different levels. There is not one silver bullet, but many good ideas that the whole community can draw on to make a difference, she suggested. Dr. Barton concluded by underscoring the need for transformational, not transactional, relationships.

MODELS FOR SYNERGISTIC PARTNERSHIPS

Workshop committee member Bryn Adams, Ph.D. (DEVCOM Army Research Laboratory), chaired a panel with three individuals who have developed synergistic partnerships in a range of settings: Kelly Freidenfelds, Ph.D. (Princeton University), Robert Shepard, Ph.D. (The Shepard Institute, LLC), and Aaron Wecksler, Ph.D. (Genentech).

Princeton Alliance for Collaborative Research and Innovation

Dr. Freidenfelds explained the Princeton Alliance for Collaborative Research and Innovation (PACRI) is a new initiative to promote research collaboration between Princeton and HBCU faculty. The first five HBCUs to participate are Howard University, Jackson State University, Spelman College, Prairie View A&M University, and University of Maryland Eastern Shore, which were identified in concert with the United Negro College Fund (UNCF). Through the program, Princeton and HBCU faculty co-submit proposals that are reviewed by reviewers from the HBCUs and Princeton. The research is funded by Princeton. There has been a strong response in engineering, natural sciences, social sciences, and humanities.

Dr. Freidenfelds works with a liaison at each school to distribute RFPs (Request for Proposals), do outreach, help with matchmaking, and recruit reviewers. The reviewers look for evidence of collaboration that would benefit researchers, students, the field, and the institutions. The funding is flexible, but common uses are for salary and course release time for the HBCU faculty, funding for graduate or postdoc students, and travel. The first 10 projects span a wide variety of topics, from coastal resilience to deepfake detection to energy storage. PACRI's central core is collaborative research that will make an impact and be innovative, she said. The hope is not only conducting the initial research but also the building of authentic relationships between Princeton and HBCU partners.

Science and Engineering Alliance

Dr. Shepard raised three issues as he described the Science and Engineering Alliance (SEA): how to ensure the equitable distribution of resources in alliances; inequities that may arise due to an imbalance; and how to bring others into an alliance, particularly 2-year colleges. SEA began in 1990 as a partnership between four HBCUs and the Lawrence

Livermore National Laboratory (LLNL) with the mission to broaden participation in the federal R&D enterprise so that the institutions could participate in large-scale projects and produce a globally competitive workforce. SEA had a board with a stand-alone office in Washington, DC. The backbone, he said, was an identification of combined and complementary technical core strengths in such areas as climate and environmental change, geographic information systems, biotechnology and biosciences, and computer and information sciences. The peer-review process was used to guide this selection.

An executive director reduced faculty workload. Over the first few months, the director's task was to educate federal agencies about what SEA could offer. Large solicitations relevant to the SEA institutions were distilled to three-page abstracts. The Washington office helped ensure that submitted proposals addressed all requirements. For each proposal, the lead institution was identified by who had the dominant strength given the specific technical area. SEA's focus on inclusion and access was reflected in the number of projects funded by the Department of Energy (DOE) and many other public, industry, and philanthropic sources, Dr. Shepard said. He called attention to two that spanned the HBCUs' technical areas: a DOE infrastructure grant and a summer internship program from LLNL. He also highlighted a Faculty Fellowship program, supported by LLNL, which was a competitive program that ran for 5 years. He noted the schools had a stake in the success; in this case, they paid for the adjunct faculty who took over the teaching during the fellowship.

For nearly 25 years, SEA engaged more than 500 HBCU and MSI faculty and garnered $350 million in new research and education funding, held four mentoring workshops, and introduced more than 400 Small Disadvantaged Businesses and Women-Owned Businesses to federal opportunities. From 1990 to 2009, the four SEA institutions totaled over $1.01 billion in combined federal support, he said. While SEA was mostly funded by LLNL, each school also paid dues based on performance.

Genentech

Dr. Wecksler spoke about interactions at Genentech with government and institutions. He said he sees relationships across sectors as a triad with government generally supporting fundamental research and industry generally funding more applied research. He noted that Genentech and other companies rely on the academic sector to understand and leverage emerging technologies. One example in biotechnology is understanding the mechanisms behind protein-based medicines, which is required by the Food and Drug Administration for drug approvals. Understanding higher-order structure is particularly complex, and a solution for Genentech was to partner with a government-funded lab, initially the Brookhaven National Laboratory. A technology called hydroxyl radical footprinting was developed after several decades of exploration and with government, industry, and university collaboration.

Genentech has several programs to foster future scientists at different levels. Internships and co-ops are available for undergraduates, a Pharmaceutical Development Rotational Program involves recent bachelor's and master's graduates, and he co-leads a postdoctoral program. To build underrepresented engagement, Dr. Wecksler said Genentech partners with Hispanic-Serving Institutions and HBCUs, as well as participates in conferences of professional societies that reach underrepresented students.

Discussion

Dr. Adams asked how to ensure the equitable distribution of resources, when in some cases, equitable does not mean equal. Dr. Shepard said these issues must be discussed at the onset of any partnership or alliance. Peer review cannot be dismissed, but it is necessary to consider how to involve weaker participants. One solution is to bring opportunities to campuses to strengthen their programs. SEA looked for solicitations that fit the technical areas of the schools with less experience and made them the lead. He pointed out the institutions did not have the same technical expertise so they could complement, not compete with, each other. SEA also focused on junior faculty and instrumentation needed for the research.

When asked about involving other institutions, Dr. Freidenfelds explained that PACRI hopes to expand but began with a proof of concept with five HBCUs based on UNCF input. She observed that academia is decentralized, and the aim is relationships to put researchers on a path to the same goal, such as joint papers, student exchanges, grant applications, or IP.

Asked for thoughts on ways to ensure and address the distribution of resources in partnerships, Dr. Wecksler commented that the Bay Area, where Genentech is located, has a number of universities. He said it is important to be an ally for those that are not the most dominant in the area so they can build capacity. Dr. Freidenfelds said she hopes Princeton is listening and supporting as best it can. She noted as an R1, Princeton can help make connections and bring partners in. Dr. Shepard said he represented a set of institutions that "are always on the hunt" in looking for resources. He has spent his career trying to convince national labs and agencies about the talent at HBCUs. He expressed hope that those that have the resources can share them.

5

Town Hall II, Day 2: True Partnerships through Institutions, a New Institute, and Federal Partnerships

Highlights from the Presentations

- By taking advantage of its location near a large Army base, Fayetteville State University is building its research portfolio. Counterparts within the University of North Carolina System have assisted with compliance and other administrative issues (Bora).
- DOD should establish a set-aside program for Tribal Colleges and Universities, as NSF and other agencies have done. This benefits both the populations that TCUs serve and the funders (Guy).
- Faculty and students understand the need for research and collaboration, but government entities need to create pathways to "enable us to get to the other side" to produce what federal agencies need (Orok).
- Regional universities offer employers talented students who want to remain in the area for their careers, which is an advantage to local industry and government facilities (Ehrman).
- The faculty at HBCUs and TCUs often have high semester teaching loads, and institutions like these have had a historical, institutional focus on teaching (Bora, Guy, Orok, Ehrman).

- Programs such as the DOE's Energy Efficiency and Renewable Energy program have found interagency agreements, for example, with NSF, maximize impact without "reinventing the wheel" (Mosley).

This list is the rapporteurs' summary of points made by the individual speakers identified, and the statements have not been endorsed or verified by the National Academies of Sciences, Engineering, and Medicine. They are not intended to reflect a consensus among workshop participants.

Day 2 of the second town hall continued to look further into true partnerships and the benefits of true partnerships to the Department of Defense (DOD), challenges to development of partnerships, and a range of successful institutional and federal agency models. The panels discussed frameworks for developing synergistic partnerships, with representatives from academia, the defense industry, and federal programs that seek to facilitate equitable government-university-industry partnerships. The first panel shared perspectives from institutions on limitations and potential investment areas for DOD funding, while another discussed federal agency programs and insights. In addition, a Historically Black Colleges and Universities (HBCUs)–focused institute focused on mathematics and computational sciences was introduced.

INSTITUTIONAL CHALLENGES TO DEVELOPING PARTNERSHIPS

Abigail Newsome, Ph.D. (Mississippi Valley State University), called attention to the challenges for all institutions to form true partnerships, and particularly for smaller institutions. She was joined by Ganesh Bora, Ph.D. (Fayetteville State University [FSU]), Elmer Guy, Ph.D. (Navajo Technical University [NTU]), Teresa Orok, Ph.D. (Alabama A&M University), and Sheryl Ehrman, Ph.D., P.E. (San José State University [SJSU]). Dr. Newsome facilitated a discussion after each introduced their institution.

Institutional Examples

Fayetteville State University

Dr. Bora noted that Fayetteville State University is located near Fort Bragg, the largest U.S. Army base in the country.[1] He outlined some of FSU's collaborations with industry and DOD, including the Army Pathfinder Program, Forward Edge-AI (artificial intelligence) (see Chapter 4), Geneva Foundation, and Fort Bragg Research Institute, as well as interaction with the DOD-HBCU coordinator in the Office of the Secretary of Defense. FSU hired recently retired Army General Michael X. Garrett as a "military executive-in-residence" to strengthen the bridge between the Army base and FSU. In addition, FSU's chief research officer connects with counterparts throughout the University of North Carolina System.

While he expressed concern about limited funding and infrastructure, he countered the perception that FSU and other HBCUs do not have expertise. FSU, like many HBCUs, began as a liberal arts institution and is struggling to build research capacity. He stressed HBCU faculty have deep expertise, but they also have heavy teaching loads. Some institutions do not have full science, technology, engineering, and mathematics (STEM) programs and/or graduate programs, but still have much to offer, he noted.

Navajo Technical University

Dr. Guy explained that Navajo Technical University is a tribal research university in the Navajo Nation in New Mexico and Arizona, with a branch campus serving the Pueblo of Zuni. (Dr. Guy also presented during the third town hall; see Chapter 6). STEM research is taking place at the undergraduate level in a number of STEM fields, with a master's in management information systems and another in electrical engineering pending approval with the Higher Learning Commission. NTU has industrial, electrical, and advanced manufacturing engineering with ABET (Accreditation Board for Engineering and Technology) accreditation.

Dr. Guy said NTU partners with mainstream institutions in Arizona, New Mexico, and beyond; with the private sector; with other Tribal Colleges and Universities (TCUs); with several HBCUs; and with the Sandia and Los Alamos National Laboratories. It is also a member of the World Indigenous Nations Higher Education Consortium. Students do capstone research

[1] Fort Bragg was renamed Fort Liberty in June 2023.

projects as individuals and in teams at labs on the NTU campuses and in internships off campus. NTU wants to expand its relationship with DOD. Two examples of support are the Hogan Project, funded by DOD, to bring high-speed wireless connectivity to NTU's Crownpoint campus and to several Navajo communities. DOD also recently helped the Advanced Manufacturing Laboratory purchase a scanning electronic microscope to support research related to DOD priorities.

Dr. Guy said a challenge is that DOD and other agencies may say that a smaller institution is not serving many students and faculty and may not want to fund equipment, yet equipment is still essential in running these types of programs. Other challenges are the amount of time needed to connect with DOD or other partners to submit proposals with limited success. NTU's research goals are to support its primary education mission, work on the cutting edge to help Navajo entrepreneurs have an advantage in the marketplace, help students enter high-skilled careers, improve the Navajo Nation through economic development, create intellectual property (IP) for the benefit of Navajo people, and provide a pathway for graduate education. One example of a research partnership is in the area of nonaqueous lithium batteries (Li-ion batteries), which are critical to clean energy and also beneficial to Navajo communities, many of whom do not have electricity. Outcomes expected are state-of-the-art research, jobs, and a battery manufacturing company. Another example is computer-aided manufacturing through the NTU Center for Advanced Manufacturing, with the research conducted via a wide range of partnerships.

NTU's goal is to build strength as a research institution and to expand its work with DOD. He urged DOD to establish a TCU set-aside, which the National Science Foundation (NSF) and other federal agencies have done. He noted TCUs tend to be small and cannot compete with larger institutions. Yet, he noted, Native Americans serve in the military at a higher rate than any other groups of Americans and strongly support the military. He added that by providing opportunities for TCUs, DOD is supporting Indian Country, while the TCUs have active research programs that can help DOD meet its priorities.

Alabama A&M University

Dr. Orok echoed the challenges expressed by other participants. She reminded the group that HBCUs were formed to serve students who were not able to participate in other universities. Instruction comes first and foremost. Looking across the landscape of HBCUs, it is important to keep in mind their diversity of size, geography, who they are serving, and whether they are public or private. These issues have a bearing on how to facilitate the research enterprise, she commented. Most do not have the level of full-time staffing needed. Faculty must take on additional responsibilities, which can inhibit research and the ability to create and sustain partnerships. Also, she noted, many HBCUs are small and located in rural communities. Many have deferred maintenance and lack labs and facilities.

Faculty and students understand the need for research and collaboration, but she urged government entities to create pathways to "enable us to get to the other side" to produce what federal agencies need. Referring to the earlier discussion about the importance of tech transfer, she observed a disconnect because most HBCUs do not have robust sponsored research staff to understand how to move the needle in this area. "What tends to happen when we enter into partnerships with major institutions, we as HBCUs and Minority-Serving Institutions (MSIs) do the work and collaborate, and at the end, others get credit for our work," she said. "There has to be a level playing ground."

HBCUs and MSIs are adept at facilitating grants, but she said the real value for impact comes from government contracts, including DOD opportunities. When she joined Alabama A&M, the university already had a separate 501(c)(3) called AAMU-RISE that provides an alternative delivery system for funding opportunities. It offers the university an opportunity to leverage research capabilities that can combine multidisciplinary strengths, including the social sciences, she explained. It provides state-of-the-art lab facilities in many areas that can compete with the top universities in the country. But looking at the entire HBCU landscape, not all institutions have these facilities. "We want to make sure as we position ourselves, we are not standing alone but are working with other MSIs. When one of us succeeds, we all succeed," Dr. Orok said. AAMU-RISE partners with government and industry, as well as with Advancing Minorities' Interest in Engineering, or AMIE, a coalition that includes fifteen HBCUs with ABET-accredited engineering programs. She briefly highlighted AAMU-RISE projects to illustrate "what can be done if HBCUs and MSIs work together and get support from DOD, with primes, with subs, and other entities that are part of the DOD landscape."

San José State University

Dr. Ehrman spoke about DOD research at regional MSIs by focusing on San José State University, one of the 23 California State Universities. (See also presentations on SJSU in Chapter 2 and Chapter 7.) She agreed with several challenges identified by other presenters, including limited faculty time for research and recognition as a supplier of workforce fed by the community college system. She noted how faculty often need to carve out resources and research time around their teaching responsibilities and concurred with Dr. Orok that they do not always get credit for their contributions. Without Ph.D.s on campus (per the California structure for higher education), it is hard to have continuity in labs. Like most low-resourced institutions, Dr. Ehrman said SJSU depends on shared facilities in the region, which are excellent but may require making appointments and waiting for access, rather than just walking down the hall. There has also been a learning curve in terms of negotiating IP with industry.

Dr. Ehrman also pointed to new opportunities. Strategies include working with faculty and program managers to understand budget requirements, looking for new sources of funding, and proactively reaching out to industry to showcase the strengths of the institution. The demographic mix of the students adds value by contributing great ideas and eventually becoming employees of local companies. She pointed to the veterans on campus, as well as students who come from places of conflict, who clearly understand the mission for U.S. security and the need to get the mission correct. To run more effectively, SJSU is using postdocs and supporting lab managers who can provide continuity with master's and bachelor's students. In addition, by involving students at community colleges before they transfer, students spend a longer time at the bench. SJSU is also looking to achieve "super user status" at regional facilities to avoid the lag time and be more efficient in instrumentation usage.

Dr. Ehrman offered four recommendations to DOD. First, she urged thinking regionally, noting that most students at regional institutions come from the region and want to stay there postgraduation, which can provide workforce. Second, long-term student engagement can be achieved through early research experiences and direction toward DOD support for graduate programs. She noted students are more aware of the area's tech companies than of DOD, and she urged DOD to be more visible. Third, she suggested support for mid-scale research instrumentation to build a body of results, including support staff to maintain them. Finally, she suggested incentives to strengthen the partnerships between research-intensive and regional institutions. MSIs could take the lead or be involved throughout a project, not just brought in to provide workforce.

Discussion

Dr. Newsome launched a short discussion by asking about resolving equity and equality at each institution. Dr. Bora noted he has worked at the National Institute for Food and Agriculture as a grant-giving body, at a large university, and now at a smaller HBCU. From the HBCU perspective, there can be collaboration at different scales, such as targeting small businesses to build a research portfolio. Dr. Orok, commenting on equity and equality, noted the good news for all MSIs when Howard University became a University Affiliated Research Center. But while it is a cause for celebration, she asked how many other MSIs are granted this level on a daily basis. "When we think about what is equitable, fair, and necessary, these are the kinds of issues we must address," she said. And although a $20 million project sounds very large, she reminded the group about the finance and administration costs, staffing, lab costs, and other expenses. Dr. Ehrman commented on mindset, noting that sometimes faculty become intimidated about submitting proposals, although this has improved in the last few years. She added that Silicon Valley has had historic discrimination in idea generation, and some students have been discouraged from pursuing STEM majors while also facing off-campus discrimination. Reaching out to community colleges is important to draw people in, she stressed.

Dr. Guy noted that TCUs have unique challenges. Many are on reservation lands based on a Trust Relationship, not ownership.[2] Because of that, it is difficult to build the infrastructure that is needed, such as faculty housing. They are building a cadre of local STEM professionals, but it will take time. One advantage of a small institution is the agility in adapting curriculum design to meet industry and community needs, which is harder in larger schools.

Dr. Orok commented about the work involved when large awards are received. Figuring out workloads and managing the process requires

[2] The "trust relationship" is a responsibility derived from federal statutes, treaties, court decisions, executive actions, and the Constitution (which assigns authority over federal-Indian relations to Congress). The provision of postsecondary education opportunities for tribal members is one manifestation of that relationship. For more information, see https://crsreports.congress.gov/product/pdf/IF/IF10554.

specialized skills according to requirements and policies. "As we step into a contractual piece, we must be clear these are contracts and not grants. The deliverables become very different. The schedule is different. If we don't manage it correctly, we get blackballed, that we can't handle the big dollars," she cautioned. Dr. Guy said NTU is just starting to win larger grants but agreed with the need to build capacity slowly. Dr. Bora said FSU works with other institutions in the state system, such as North Carolina State University, to help with compliance and related issues.

To set up and measure successful research partnerships, it is important to share expertise to solve community problems, Dr. Bora suggested. Dr. Ehrman said a successful partnership is one in which the entities are truly partners, rather than "industry just throwing money over the fence." One example is when students can work directly with an industry collaborator and faculty. Sometimes it takes a while to work out the details. Dr. Guy concurred that the partnerships that are most successful take time to develop, and Dr. Orok added that partnerships are a two-way street. Minority Institutions must position themselves to have an impactful and sustainable relationship with partners to acquire funding and place students. She also said if missions are not aligned, it may be necessary to stop them.

When asked by Dr. Newsome for one idea that each would change with a magic wand, Dr. Ehrman replied that she wished for better utilized space. Dr. Bora called for more resources for the labs to serve communities. Dr. Guy expressed the wish to do more work with the Navajo government on economic development. Dr. Orok said she would wish for agencies to establish technical support centers to enable institutions to systematically go after awards more competitively and provide guidance that institutions need.

APPLIED RESEARCH INSTITUTE FOR MATHEMATICS AND COMPUTATIONAL SCIENCES

Chad Womack, Ph.D. (United Negro College Fund [UNCF]) discussed the Applied Research Institute for Mathematics and Computational Sciences (ARI), a new initiative that emerged from work by UNCF, the Thurgood Marshall College Fund, presidents at HBCUs, and Google. Dr. Womack called on the African proverb "If you want to go fast, go alone. If you want to go far, go together." In this context, Dr. Womack said, ARI is a "go-together strategy. This is about how do we bring our respective institutions together on a platform that will support and enhance their research profiles and capacities in the mathematics and computational sciences." He acknowledged the contributions of colleagues who were involved in the development of ARI over more than a year.

The first step, he explained, was to look at data to understand what research in these fields was taking place at HBCUs. This was done by mining the NSF database of active research awards on key words (e.g., AI [artificial intelligence], deep learning, machine learning). A more comprehensive study of NSF awards is under way.

The vision for ARI is "to establish an HBCU-anchored institute that conducts leading-edge applied research in a variety of mathematical and computational fields and produce commercially applicable solutions that have positive social impact." A foundational principle, he stressed, is the belief that solutions can be developed that are technologically advanced with positive social impact. In addition to building and sustaining research capacity, ARI is designed to strengthen innovative pedagogy so that students learn cutting-edge knowledge. Thus, the key priorities are to (1) build math and computer science research and teaching capacity at HBCUs, (2) (re)build the research and academic talent pipeline, and (3) build tech entrepreneurship and commercialization capacity at HBCUs.

The core of the model is what is called the ARI Triad, in which HBCU research networks and communities are linked to Tier 1 academic research partners and companies (see Figure 5-1). The first such partner is Google, he announced.

Pilot research awards will go to faculty, who will then be eligible for a higher level of project funding. At each level, the vision is to provide catalytic support to work on ideas and build solutions to faculty, affinity groups, and research communities. A workshop model pioneered by Fay Cobb Payton, Ph.D., will help faculty put together highly competitive proposals for ARI but also for other external funding. ARI will be organized through research affinity groups and networks so that HBCU faculty and students with interest in certain verticals (e.g., computational biology) organize to create research communities. As they receive resources and get to know each other, they become potential research partners that can partner with companies and Tier 1 institutions. Students are at the core of these communities.

Dr. Womack expressed excitement that ARI is progressing beyond the concept stage and is working with partners and stakeholders. An advisory board is being formed to support HBCUs.

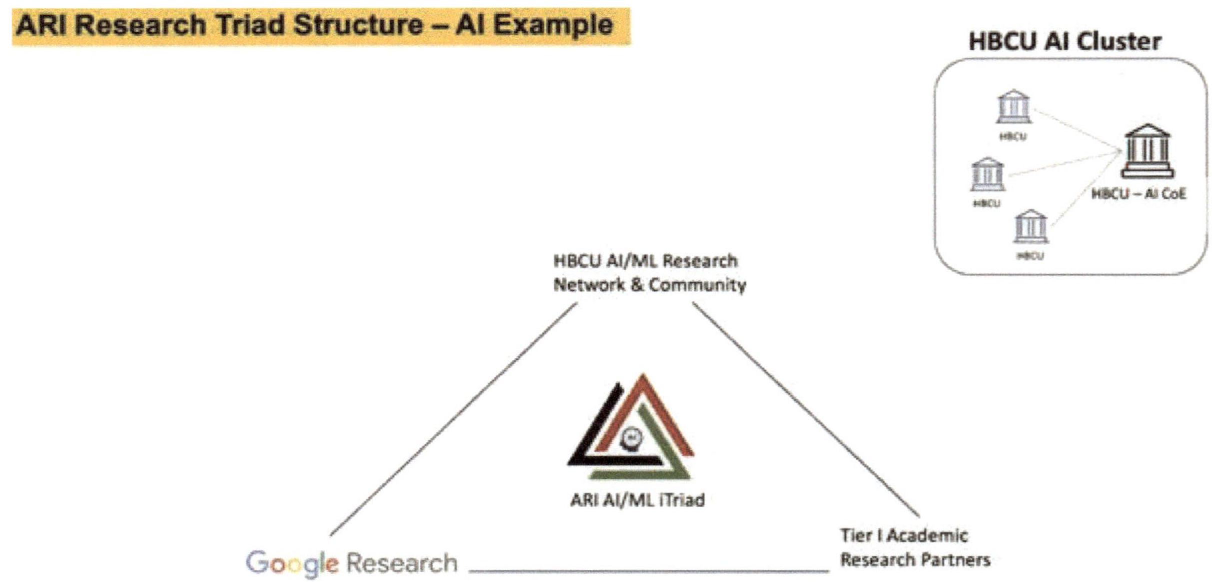

FIGURE 5-1 ARI Research Triad, with AI as an example.
SOURCE: Chad Womack, Town Hall Presentation, May 23, 2023.

Discussion

Workshop chair Oscar Barton, Jr., Ph.D., P.E. (Morgan State University), pointed to ARI's potential to impact curricula, including delivering curricula through different modalities. He urged working with deans to build in flexibility. An ABET-accredited degree sets requirements, and electives have morphed into requirements in some programs, he observed. Dr. Womack agreed with the challenge to make innovative changes in core curricula. In forming ARI, these issues were addressed with the idea of bringing in research and pedagogy to support schools. "Our goal is to support you to offer cutting-edge curricula to students, in a way that builds capacity—not to subtract, but to add," Dr. Womack stressed. For example, he expressed hope that postgraduate fellows supported by ARI may work at HBCUs. Another idea, suggested by Dr. Newsome, is to build modules embedded within existing courses that could excite students, faculty, and administration. She also suggested credentialing for teachers who go through ARI programs.

Several participants asked how the ARI model might be exported to other MSIs, as well as to a range of industrial and academic partners. Another expressed concern that ARI's research award model does not provide sufficient support in the pilot stage for faculty buyouts, which have been identified as a challenge. He also commented that curricula changes can take years. Dr. Womack said ARI is an affiliated communal research asset for HBCUs and welcomes new participants. Research faculty may be offered joint appointments with ARI to provide flexibility. He acknowledged the pilot stage does not provide enough funding for buyouts, but noted most faculty are on 9-month appointments, and this stage is envisioned to take place during the summer. ARI envisions building up both a research and a teaching core, to alleviate the stress around a department's fear of losing teaching capacity. He urged lifting up teaching and pedagogy to make sure faculty who prioritize teaching are resourced. What distinguishes HBCUs from Predominantly White Institutions, or PWIs, is the great teaching that is culturally responsive, Dr. Womack said, but it is also important to support faculty members with deep research interests.

FEDERAL PARTNERSHIP PROGRAMS

The final session of the second town hall focused on federal agency programs that have successfully facilitated the development of equitable partnerships. Moderated by Keith McGee, Ph.D. (Alcorn State University), the presenters were Jesus Soriano Molla, Ph.D. (National Science Foundation), and Terrence Mosley (Department of Energy [DOE]). The opportunities they discussed are in addition to others described by their agency colleagues at the first and third town halls (see Chapters 3 and 7).

National Science Foundation TIP Directorate

Dr. Soriano provided an overview of NSF programs that accelerate research to impact, with a focus on NSF's Directorate for Technology, Innovation, and Partnerships (TIP), and invited participants to see which are most relevant to their needs. TIP is creating horizontal approaches in collaboration with other directorates to achieve the NSF mission to promote the progress of science; secure the national defense; and advance the national health, prosperity, and welfare, he explained. The three approaches are to (1) foster innovation and technology ecosystems, (2) establish translation pathways, and (3) partner to engage the nation's diverse talent.

While NSF has a budget of $10 billion and supports 350,000 individuals from undergraduate to faculty levels, millions of people are not participating in NSF or the STEM enterprise in general, and such challenges as climate change and access to health care need their talent, he said. One way that NSF has determined it can involve more Americans is through partnerships. A marquee TIP program is the creation of regional innovation engines to develop a range of partners to engage in use-inspired research, drive research results to the market and society, promote workforce development, and stimulate the economy and create jobs. Forty-three development awards were recently made.[3]

Dr. Soriano highlighted a number of other TIP-coordinated programs:

- Enabling Partnerships to Increase Innovation Capacity, or EPIC, which provides training and networking support to help build more inclusive innovation ecosystems and a pathway into larger NSF Regional Innovation Engines, with up to $400,000 for 3 years.
- Convergence Accelerator program, which brings together multidisciplinary teams to stimulate idea sharing and development of sustainable solutions.

[3] For more information on the development of NSF Regional Innovation Engines and for the programs listed below, see beta.nsf.gov/tip/latest.

- Small Business Innovation Research grants, which help bridge the "valley of death" between research and commercialization.
- Partnerships for Innovation, which support faculty to do proof-of-concept work, ideally in partnership with industry or national labs.
- Innovation Corps, or I-Corps, which trains NSF-funded faculty, students, and other researchers in innovation and entrepreneurship skills.
- Pathways to Enable Open-Source Ecosystems, or POSE, which supports the creation of open-source platforms to promote new technology solutions.
- Accelerating Research Translation, or ART, which provides $6 million for up to 4 years to build capacity to strengthen and scale the translation of basic research outcomes into impactful solutions.
- Visionary Interdisciplinary Teams Advancing Learning, or VITAL, which is a prize challenge to develop innovate learning technology for K–12 students.
- Experiential Learning for Emerging and Novel Technologies, or ExLENT, which is a workforce development program that promotes partnerships between organizations in emerging technology fields and those with expertise in workforce development.
- Activate, which is an entrepreneurial fellowship program that supports researchers from a variety of backgrounds and geographies to move technologies from lab to society.

As TIP ramps up, Dr. Soriano invited participants to learn about the program and funding opportunities most relevant to their needs and to participate.

Department of Energy's Energy Efficiency and Renewable Energy

Mr. Mosley spoke about partnership programs with DOE's Energy Efficiency and Renewable Energy (EERE). The mission of EERE is to accelerate the research, development, demonstration, and deployment of technologies and solutions to equitably transition America to net-zero greenhouse gas emissions by no later than 2050. There is an emphasis on workers and communities who have been most negatively impacted by the energy transition and those historically underserved by the energy system and overburdened by pollution.

An interagency agreement with NSF is an opportunity for EERE to take advantage of established programs to broaden STEM participation beyond its traditional research and development (R&D) audience. A 5-year, $50 million program will provide technical training, K–12 outreach, and other efforts to interest a range of people in clean energy. As one example of the use of the interagency agreement, EERE is taking advantage of an NSF internship program in geothermal energy. A partnership with NSF's Engineering Research Initiation program will fund researchers at non-R1 institutions. As noted by Dr. Soriano, NSF has begun many programs through the CHIPS + Science Act, and the opportunities are great. EERE also takes part in the MSI STEM R&D Consortium (MSRDC), which consists of more than 70 MSIs and is aimed at reducing barriers to entry for MSIs to do more research for DOE and other agencies.[4,5] In FY 2022, EERE funded $8.6 million in direct R&D funding through the consortium. Of note, the partnership developed when he met MSRDC representatives at a National Academies of Sciences, Engineering, and Medicine workshop.

EERE recently launched the HBCU Clean Energy Education Prize, which has two tracks. The Inspire Track funds HBCU-hosted programs for K–12 and/or community college students. The Partnerships Track gives HBCUs the opportunity to develop new partnerships to equip HBCU students with the skills to succeed in clean energy careers. The partnerships are designed to enhance existing opportunities such as exchange programs, online offerings, and the transition of MSI students to graduate school or careers.[6]

The work is paying off for DOE and MSIs, Mr. Mosley said. In 2022, DOE was ranked third as a top HBCU supporter among government agencies and nonprofits, yet it was not even in the top 10 agencies in 2020, according to the Career Communications Group, Inc. Mr. Mosley concluded, "Through partnerships, we can lean on each other to get the best results and reach concurrent goals."

Discussion

To further discuss how federal agencies are interacting with MSIs, Mr. Mosley described MBE (Minority Business Enterprises) Connect, a DOE

[4] For more information, see https://www.congress.gov/bill/117th-congress/house-bill/4346.

[5] For more information, see https://www.msrdconsortium.org.

[6] For more information, see https://www.herox.com/HBCU.

summit held in February 2022. MSI representatives talked with DOE staff to review funding opportunities. In addition, the DOE Office of Economic Impact and Diversity started a webinar series with MSIs to learn about current and upcoming funding opportunities and to help connect them to the right offices. He reinforced the need for advocacy, developing strategic partnerships, and not "re-creating the wheel."

While many programs require partnerships, Dr. Soriano acknowledged that some institutions need the tools to initiate and sustain them. He encouraged MSIs to advocate and engage agencies to focus on these tools, something that TIP is starting to do. He also pointed to the INCLUDES Initiative as an opportunity in this respect.[7]

Both Dr. Soriano and Mr. Mosley underscored the need for evaluation and tracking. At NSF, according to Dr. Soriano, a centralized group is developing intentional evaluations to assess the success of partnership creation and factors involved in success or failures. At DOE, according to Mr. Mosley, a strategic analysis group is evaluating several programs to measure impact, such as a solar decathlon that has been going on for about 20 years. Both stressed the need to reach K–12 students to interest them in STEM.

[7] For more information, see https://new.nsf.gov/funding/opportunities/inclusion-across-nation-communities-learners.

6

Town Hall III, Day 1: Research Activity, Recruitment, and Administrative Bandwidth

Highlights from the Presentations

- Helpful support to take on more research activity could include core equipment funding, fellowships/stipends for increasing Ph.D. capacity, seed funding for partnerships, funding for research development and administration, and support so that research-active distinguished faculty can provide mentoring to junior faculty (Wesson).
- True partnerships could be strengthened by inviting minority institutions' vice presidents of research (MI VPR) to serve on relevant DOD committees and working groups and placing Defense Research Capacity Liaison Officers in MI VPR offices (Wilson).
- Useful support from federal agencies could include resources to recruit top-quality graduate students who, in turn, would support faculty in their research (Armwood-Gordon).
- Faculty need training to understand the cost structure of grants and contracts and the impact of facilities and administrative costs on the institution (Collins).
- Providing broadband through Internet to the Hogan, funded by DOD and the state of New Mexico, jumpstarted the research program at Navajo Tech (Guy).

This list is the rapporteurs' summary of points made by the individual speakers identified, and the statements have not been endorsed or verified by the National Academies of Sciences, Engineering, and Medicine. They are not intended to reflect a consensus among workshop participants.

The third town hall took place in Chicago, Illinois, on June 28–29, 2023. It highlighted existing administrative structures that can facilitate and sustain research and explored how the Department of Defense (DOD) and other agencies can support trainees and faculty across the research ecosystem.

TRANSITIONING FROM LOW TO HIGH RESEARCH ACTIVITY

The first panel, moderated by workshop committee member Thomas Tubon, Ph.D. (BioMADE), focused on how two institutions have transitioned to take on more research activity. The speakers were Rosemarie Wesson, Ph.D. (City College of New York [CCNY]), and Gillian Wilson, Ph.D. (University of California, Merced [UC Merced]).

City College of New York

Dr. Wesson began by explaining that the City College of New York, founded in 1847, is the initial institution of what is now the City University of New York (CUNY). CCNY has eight schools and divisions, each involved in research in some way, and educates more than 15,000 undergraduate and graduate students who come from families that speak more than 80 languages. It is one of CUNY's 25 campuses across New York's five boroughs.

CCNY is an R2 institution with 450 student researchers across disciplines, including undergraduates, graduates, and postdocs. Dr. Wesson noted that bolstering organizational charts that have limited staff support, like CCNY's, would strengthen research capacity. CCNY has one director of research development, one research manager, and one director of research compliance, and they are hiring an assistant director of proposal development. The grants and sponsored programs research office has 15 full-time equivalent staff. Awards and expenditures have grown from about $55 million in 2017 to $72 million in 2022. The relatively slow growth, she noted, is somewhat by design. Most comes from federal sources, but also city, state, private, and CUNY sources.

With limited resources, Dr. Wesson said strategies to grow research are to identify and communicate research strengths and emerging opportunities; encourage internal and external collaboration; focus on junior faculty; reach out to prospective faculty; use Pivot, an electronic funding software; pursue targeted announcements of limited submission/Minority-Serving Institution (MSI) opportunities; and share research accomplishments. She described each strategy briefly.

After numerous meetings, CCNY strengths have been identified in which a critical mass of researchers are engaged and opportunities are emerging, which is termed QC-ALERT (quantum research, cybersecurity, artificial intelligence, life sciences, energy and the environment, robotics, and transportation). Collaboration across disciplines has been encouraged through internal seed funding. For example, a Climate Solidarity team encompassing science, engineering, architecture, and sociology received a seed award. Focusing on faculty includes discussing research areas of interest with prospective faculty so they know about CUNY collaborative opportunities. A boot camp for junior faculty has been established to strengthen grant-writing skills. Since starting the camp, faculty have received eight National Science Foundation (NSF) and two Department of Energy awards. PIVOT has been introduced to all faculty with training so that they can search for funding that fits their expertise. Limited submission awards are targeted to relevant faculty. They receive help to build a proposal and barriers are removed as much as possible so that they can focus on the research. Finally, an electronic magazine spotlights faculty and their research successes.

Dr. Wesson offered several recommendations for increased Historically Black College and University (HBCU)/MSI research activity. She reiterated the value of meaningful collaborations, as well as core equipment funding that includes funding for support personnel, fellowships/stipends for increasing Ph.D. capacity, seed funding for partnerships, funding for research development and administration, and support so that research-active distinguished faculty can provide mentoring to junior faculty. She stressed that one size does not fit all. Community and the strengths of faculty members must be considered at different institutions, she concluded.

University of California, Merced

Dr. Wilson oversees research, innovation, and economic development, which she said is slightly unusual but not unique to combine these three areas at an institution. The University of California, Merced, was established in 2005 to "address chronically low levels of educational attainment in the region" in the rural, traditionally underserved Central Valley of the state. It is a Hispanic-Serving Institution (HSI) and an Asian American and Native American Pacific Islander–Serving Institution (AANAPISI), with almost the entire student population from California and 67 percent first-generation students. Within 11 years, it became an R2 institution and is considered an emerging research institution.

Dr. Wilson concurred with the 2022 National Academies of Sciences, Engineering, and Medicine consensus study report *Defense Research Capacity at Historically Black Colleges and Universities and Other Minority Institutions: Transitioning from Good Intentions to Measurable Outcomes*, noting that it summed up well what MSIs can contribute to DOD and how their capabilities can be more fully utilized. She noted the report highlights the variety across institutions (NASEM, 2022), but also shared characteristics, including having a disproportionately large impact to develop a diverse graduate student pool and workforce, prioritizing a culture of serving students, receiving less funding and endowments, and promoting service to communities. Half of the UC Merced campus has been built since 2018, and it is a "start-up on an incredible trajectory," she said. Many early-career faculty must be brought up to speed, but, she said, this provides tremendous opportunity for development. It has been successful in obtaining Defense University Research Instrumentation Program, or DURIP, and Multidisciplinary University Research Initiatives, or MURI, funding. Research funding has tripled since 2020. "I would argue that by partnering with an institution with a profile like ours, the nation reaps a double return," Wilson said, citing the benefit of greater diversity in the workforce and the impact of the research itself.

"We are driving hard to get to R1 without losing our HSI identity," Dr. Wilson said. The state has invested in the institution in such areas as climate action, agriculture, health innovations, and natural resources. Dr. Wilson noted the advantages of being part of the UC System, which includes three national labs. Discussions have been held about becoming involved in restricted research, which is not currently carried out on UC campuses.

To form true partnerships, she suggested inviting minority institutions' vice presidents of research (MI VPRs) to serve on relevant committees and working groups, placing Defense Research Capacity Liaison Officers in MI VPR offices, faculty cluster hires, and support for infrastructure. With a very lean staff, she called attention to the NSF GRANTED (Growing Research Access for Nationally Transformative Equity and Diversity) program as a model to support capacity at emerging research institutions. (See Chapter 3 for a presentation on GRANTED.)

Discussion

Dr. Tubon commented that DOD has many programs, but they are sometimes hard to understand and access. Dr. Wilson noted that in working with DOD, personal relationships matter to learn about opportunities and how to access them. Two solutions she suggested were for DOD personnel to spend time with early-career faculty or serve as on-campus liaisons. Dr. Wesson agreed and stressed the value of early connections. "What we find is when an announcement comes out, it is already too late," she said. Dr. Tubon underscored that some programs have a short response time that requires a rapid pivot. Dr. Wesson said when a solicitation is announced, especially for larger opportunities, there is not enough time to begin a collaboration or start a proposal. It is important to anticipate and plan for upcoming opportunities. She also urged better ways to communicate with funding agencies about an institution's strengths to ask if anything relevant is planned that would need those strengths. "Sometime, if you don't ask, you don't know," she commented. Dr. Wilson said it is important to "get upstream" of funding opportunities. It is also important to get faculty in the decision-making process, not just as responders. Dr. Tubon agreed that better two-way communication could build MI capacity.

Responding to a question from workshop committee member Abraham Wolcott, Ph.D. (San José State University), Dr. Wesson said CUNY has moved from primarily an undergraduate to a doctoral R2 institution, and the leadership must show New York State and New York City policymakers that CCNY is research-active through a long-term effort. Dr. Wilson commented, "We are in the education and research business. It is to the nation's benefit to have diverse institutions who are doing incredible work with both missions." Committee chair Oscar Barton, Jr., Ph.D., P.E. (Morgan State University), noted the American College of Education has information and resources on transitioning through the Carnegie Classification system.[1]

---

[1] For more information, see https://carnegieclassifications.acenet.edu/?_ga=2.227430045.1284099891.1694460596-385182587.1694460596.

RECRUITING RESEARCH-CENTERED FACULTY AT NON-R1 INSTITUTIONS

Faculty working at non-R1 schools are conducting cutting-edge research, noted Chad Womack, Ph.D. (United Negro College Fund). He moderated a panel in which Joanna Brooks, Ph.D. (San Diego State University [SDSU]), Catherine Armwood-Gordon, Ph.D. (Tennessee State University [TSU]), and Ivan Mosley, Ph.D. (Tennessee State University), described how faculty and trainees are recruited to come to their institutions.

San Diego State University

Dr. Brooks described San Diego State University's Building on Inclusive Excellence in Research (BIE), which is a recruiting program that intersects with the goal of becoming an R1 institution.[2] As background, SDSU is part of the California State University system and has about 31,000 undergraduate and 4,700 graduate students; it is an HSI and an AANAPISI. Under the SDSU president, research has become an important part of the institution's self-conception with the goal to become an HSI R1 public university.[3] She underscored the asset-based approach articulated in the strategic plan, including building on SDSU's historic mission and values; geographic location; connection with Latinx, Indigenous, AANAPISI, and other BIPOC (Black, Indigenous, People of Color) communities; and strengths in education, public health, and ecology/biology/biotech. She noted recognizing these assets influences how SDSU hires new faculty.

The challenge is to recruit "where excellence and access converge," Dr. Brooks said. It is important to recruit faculty whose research can capitalize on SDSU's assets while extending specific benefits to the diverse student body. Constraints based on California's Proposition 209 have pushed SDSU to explore how to institutionalize these commitments in hiring criteria, including criteria around research.[4] This exploration led to the creation of the BIE program in 2016 and its campuswide expansion in 2019 (see Figure 6-1). She noted that the model was developed by the Center for the Advancement of Multicultural Perspectives on Science, or CAMPOS, at the University of California, Davis.

---

[2] For more information on BIE, see https://sacd.sdsu.edu/cie/bie.

[3] To view the SDSU strategic plan, see https://www.sdsu.edu/strategic-plan.

[4] For more information, see https://lao.ca.gov/ballot/1996/prop209_11_1996.html.

The BIE program at SDSU began in 2016–2017 when the provost and senate set aside four additional lines for candidates in regular searches who met the criteria. This incentivized search committees to "try on" the criteria as they reviewed their pool of candidates. It was extended to all searches as a baseline expectation in 2019–2020. It was amplified in 2020–2021 with a cluster hire that particularized the BIE criteria to African American communities in an array of fields with critical research needs (e.g., public health, social work, and education). As an outcome of the program, underrepresented faculty went from 13 percent of the 2016 cohort to 48 to 52 percent in 2021–2022.

Dr. Brooks stressed that hiring with the BIE criteria in mind has led to research aligned with SDSU's assets and excellence goals. "It's a matter of finding the right process and the right alignment so the faculty we are bringing in are building on our assets as they continue their research endeavors," she said.

Tennessee State University

Dr. Armwood-Gordon spoke about recruitment in the engineering programs at Tennessee State University. There are 43 faculty members and 110 students in the graduate program, with a goal to increase the number of graduate students to support faculty research. One obstacle is limited faculty start-up funds. As chair of the civil and architectural engineering department, she worked to make faculty feel supported through a mentorship program, leveraging new faculty into proposals, equipment, and as much course release time or other support as possible. Before TSU became an R2, faculty taught four classes per semester, which has been reduced to three; internally, she looks for ways to lighten the load further for new faculty.

Dr. Armwood-Gordon also looks to leverage the ability to collaborate with industry and national labs. A new engineering building with adjustable space is being planned, which has also helped with recruiting. She noted she is trying to develop more cohesive policies across the college of engineering.

Dr. Mosley added his perspective from TSU's Department of Applied and Industrial Technologies, which has the Aviation Management and Mechatronics programs. The focus is on partnerships with industry and a hands-on approach in the curriculum. Related to recruitment, the skill set is changing rapidly, with an emphasis on working in teams.

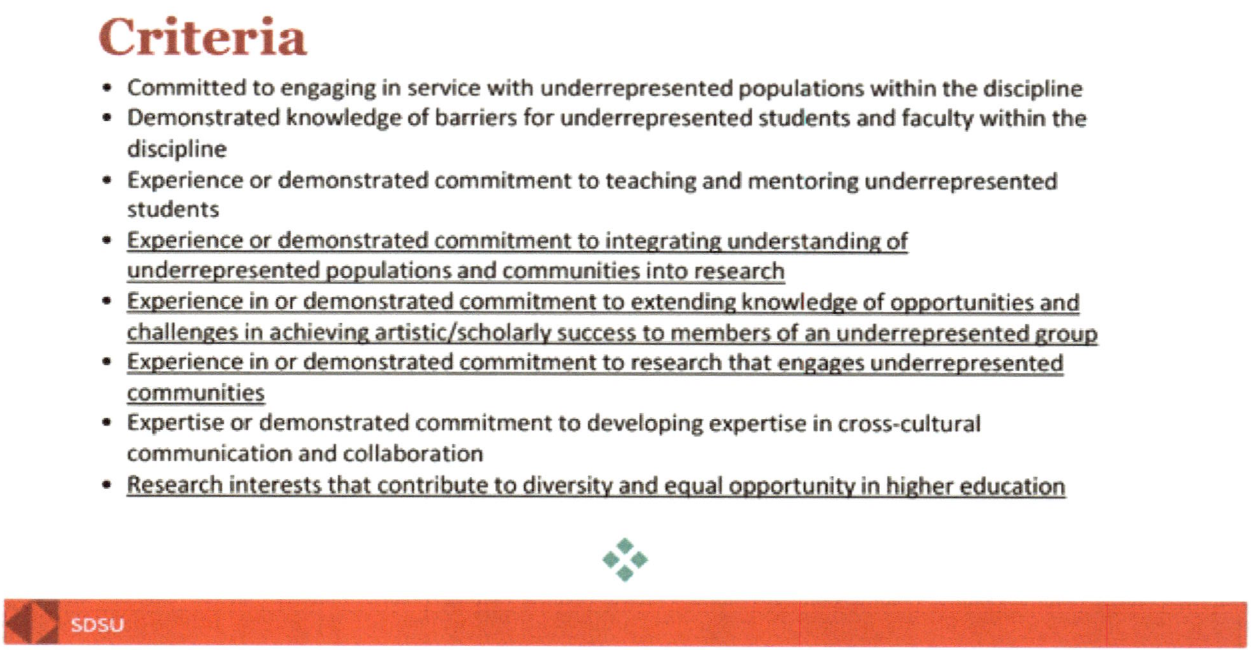

FIGURE 6-1 Building on Inclusive Excellence criteria.
SOURCE: Joanna Brooks, Town Hall Presentation, June 26, 2023.

Discussion

Dr. Womack asked how talent is recruited from graduate to postdoc to faculty levels, and how to recruit and retain freshly minted Ph.D.s. Dr. Brooks said SDSU draws from resources from the National Center for Faculty Diversity and Development.[5] It centers faculty development on the default assumption that the new person is a woman of color and looks for ways to make the environment more welcoming. For example, a survey showed SDSU women faculty of color were experiencing compromised health outcomes from stress, and supports have been provided. The area's high housing prices are the top reason for non-retention of faculty, she added. Dr. Armwood-Gordon echoed that housing costs have a negative impact on recruiting young faculty and postdocs at TSU. They do receive many applications for each vacancy, mostly from international candidates, and one goal is to increase the number of U.S. faculty. Mentorship and a supportive, non-siloed environment are beneficial to younger faculty. She acknowledged that even with these efforts, some are recruited to larger institutions based on their TSU accomplishments.

To ensure the blend of research, experience, and ability to identify needed student interventions, Dr. Mosley responded that faculty need hands-on experience. They can be assisted in searching for grants if they do not have this background, and new faculty are encouraged to turn their dissertations into publications. In terms of tenure policies, Dr. Armwood-Gordon noted both university and college policies. The university has recently made stipends available for particularly effective research. Dr. Brooks said SDSU's approach to reappointment, tenure, and promotion has shifted to provide more clarity and transparency to become more of a development process than a punitive one.

In response to a question from Dr. Barton, Dr. Brooks discussed SDSU's BIE criteria in greater detail. She reiterated that the initial criteria came from UC Davis, and the challenge is to implement them. Part of the process is a peer-review step to ensure that the candidates being put forward as finalists do meet the criteria. That led to some friction at first, she said, because faculty outside a department would be providing input. Over time, they refined the process, including guidance for international candidates and the extra layer of peer review.

Dr. Wolcott asked Dr. Armwood-Gordon if a federal agency like DOD or NSF could create a program for recruitment, what she would like it to

[5] For information, see https://www.facultydiversity.org.

look like. She noted hard funds to include resources for equipment. She also suggested the value of a package that supports graduate students—either funding for individual students or more proactively by building a graduate program that prospective faculty can see will be available to them. Among some recent faculty who left, an issue was their ability to recruit graduate students for their research, particularly Ph.D. students.

ADAPTING ADMINISTRATIVE BANDWIDTH FOR INCREASED RESEARCH ACTIVITY

An important ingredient to expand the "bandwidth" for research is to build the supporting infrastructure and to overcome administrative hurdles, noted Dr. Wolcott. He facilitated a panel on this topic composed of Almesha Campbell, Ph.D. (Jackson State University [JSU]), Laura Collins, Ph.D. (North Carolina Agricultural and Technical State University [N.C. A&T]), and Elmer Guy, Ph.D. (Navajo Technical University [NTU]).

Jackson State University

Dr. Campbell noted that Jackson State University's Division of Research has been reduced because of lower state support and other financial strains. For example, there were three assistant vice presidents when she joined the division 14 years ago, and she is now the only one. When Vice President for Research Joseph Whittaker came 5 years ago, he evaluated each person to understand how each could contribute to a robust research enterprise. Extensive cross-training occurred. Compliance was determined to be a major issue, and it was decided to take the burden from researchers as much as possible, which meant ensuring the division has the necessary training and resources to be more efficient. Platforms have been instituted to make the process more seamless for faculty. When a faculty member submits a proposal, compliance needs are automatically triggered, for example, related to human subjects research. She underscored the strong relationship between her office and faculty. Her office responds to every communication with urgency, and if a request cannot be supported, explains why. As a result, she said, the faculty feels more comfortable with her office's processes.

Dr. Campbell expressed thanks to the federal agencies for programs for MSIs and HBCUs to help build capacity, such as the National Institutes of Health (NIH) Pathways to Excellence and Innovation (PIE) to improve development of capability statements, pricing, and contracts. All staff participated in this training.[6]

North Carolina Agricultural and Technical State University

Dr. Collins said North Carolina Agricultural and Technical State University has increased its research portfolio by the number of full proposals submitted and awards received. For administration, the workload is often commensurate if an award is small or large, but researchers are going after and receiving larger award amounts. Sharing an organizational chart of N.C. A&T's Division of Research and Administration, she noted a number of vacant positions and recently filled positions that have required training. She is the only staff member assigned to tech transfer.

While MSIs have a strong reputation of "punching above their weight," Dr. Collins noted they often receive less funding from foundations and other sources than other institutions. She echoed the value of the NIH PIE grants, as well as training from the National Organization of Research Development Professionals, or NORDP, and NSF's GRANTED program. Additional funding provides access to more resources, including consulting services, research administration systems, and assistance to faculty to identify opportunities that align with their strengths and interests. Research librarians can provide valuable input. She stressed that faculty and administrators form a team. It is important to engage with junior faculty in particular, such as helping them develop stronger proposals, understand how to use feedback for future submissions, build internal and external relationships, participate in review panels, and build on successes. Administrators at all levels should instruct and advocate for institutional research strengths and priorities with legislators, agencies, and others.

She noted prospective partners often contact them, but it is important to confirm fit and alignment and not just "chase shiny things." As others have brought up, Dr. Collins warned against so-called partners who parachute in at the last minute seeking a letter of support compared with those who want to grow an intentional relationship.

Dr. Collins also underscored important elements in conversations with faculty: the importance of negotiations for projects with facilities and administration (F&A) costs as full as possible, the impact of cost-sharing

---

[6] For more information, see oamp.od.nih.gov/nih-small-business-program-office/nih-path-to-excellence-innovation-initiative.

arrangements, and an understanding of how research funds are spent on campus.

Navajo Technical University

Dr. Guy explained that NTU began as workforce development project offering certificate programs tied to jobs available in or near the Navajo Nation and has grown since 1979. (See also Dr. Guy's presentation in Chapter 5.) Research is a key component to this growth and to economic development, he said. New science, technology, engineering, and mathematics degrees were created, first at the associate's level. Administrators and key staff developed a vision through strategic planning; work groups; and engagement with students, the community, and other stakeholders, he explained. Several special projects were begun with the supercomputing community. DOD and the state of New Mexico provided support to bring broadband to the campus. The excitement of this project, known as Internet for the Hogan, inspired other programs, including NASA grants and baccalaureate degrees in information technology, advanced manufacturing, and culinary arts. Faculty credentials have been strengthened, with a policy to seek funding for faculty to earn advanced degrees. New faculty were hired who had advanced degrees and new labs were created. The journey has taken decades, but NTU now generates millions of dollars in research funding, and currently has 81 active grants and multiple university partners across the United States. It all starts with a vision and people willing to work together for the greater purpose, Dr. Guy stressed.

Discussion

Dr. Wolcott followed up with the presenters. Although the panel was entitled "administrative bandwidth," Dr. Wolcott commented that it took Internet bandwidth at NTU to build the research program. Dr. Guy agreed that high-speed broadband enhanced the capabilities of the institution and attracted students, especially in an area where some people do not have running water or electricity.

Regarding overlapping skill sets at JSU, Dr. Campbell said it is necessary to be innovative. For example, a recent DOD award included funding for a contract specialist. An NSF Engine Award was used to build tech transfer capabilities. She said partnerships must be strategic and intentional. She warned against burning out faculty and looking out for them in their tenure and promotion processes. Her office tries to be champions for faculty. Concurring with Dr. Collins, she said that JSU faculty are encouraged to request full F&A, and a range of incentives is provided when they submit proposals.

Dr. Collins said in considering partnerships, it is important that there is a champion on campus and that it aligns with priorities. Regarding cost sharing, Dr. Campbell noted that projects that require university matching funds can be huge burdens, especially for MSIs without large foundations. Another participant noted that arts and humanities projects are important to contribute to national security, but many funding agencies in these areas require cost sharing that is difficult to meet. Dr. Guy said his institution advocates for waiving cost sharing where possible.

Dr. Barton concluded that the discussion shows the necessity not only of financial but also human capital. Looking across the institutions discussed during the day, CCNY and UC Merced recognized the business aspects involved. TSU and SDSU identified important issues related to recruitment and retention, with criteria for faculty hiring. Guidance to researchers is essential, as shown in the last panel.

REFERENCE

NASEM (National Academies of Sciences, Engineering, and Medicine). 2022. *Defense Research Capacity at Historically Black Colleges and Universities and Other Minority Institutions: Transitioning from Good Intentions to Measurable Outcomes*. Washington, DC: The National Academies Press.

7

Town Hall III, Day 2: Workforce Pipeline, Engaging in Federally Funded Research, Capacity Building, and Final Thoughts

Highlights from the Presentations

- The value proposition to invest in the 2- to 4-year transfer pipeline stems from the fact that more than 40 percent of U.S. undergraduates matriculate in community colleges, a disproportionate number of whom are from underserved and minoritized communities (Hilker-Balkissoon).
- Student research positions need to pay students a competitive hourly wage or they will pass up these opportunities out of a need to earn money (Keith).
- Steps that DOD might take include requiring universities to acknowledge awarded faculty, posting changes in HBCU/MI award criteria in advance, openly disclosing changes in allowable costs, assigning specific program managers to enhance communication, and creating DOD-based training programs similar to NIH's MARC and RISE programs (Wolcott).
- Focusing on graduate recruitment within the institution, by encouraging current undergraduate and master's students to consider doctoral study, benefits students, faculty, and the institution (Zein-Sabatto).
- NSF, NIH, and DOE's Sandia Lab have programs for graduate students, faculty, and institutions that can serve as models for other funding agencies (Norman, Koduri, Treadwell).

This list is the rapporteurs' summary of points made by the individual speakers identified, and the statements have not been endorsed or verified by the National Academies of Sciences, Engineering, and Medicine. They are not intended to reflect a consensus among workshop participants.

The final day of the town hall series began with introductions of committee members and presenters who were attending the Chicago, Illinois, meeting in person, before moving on to three panels and a wrap-up discussion.

BARRIERS TO EXPANDING THE DEFENSE RESEARCH WORKFORCE PIPELINE

Workshop committee member Bryn Adams, Ph.D. (DEVCOM Army Research Laboratory), said her recognition of the need to expand awareness among U.S. citizens from diverse backgrounds to understand Department of Defense (DOD) opportunities was strengthened when she participated in a 1-year detail at the Pentagon on workforce development. The pipeline can provide highly successful careers, she said. Discussing ways to strengthen this pipeline were Shannon Arnold, M.Eng., M.S. (GBL Systems Corporation), Kerin Hilker-Balkissoon, Ph.D. (George Mason University [GMU]), Charlene Mello, Ph.D. (University of Massachusetts Dartmouth [UMass Dartmouth]), and Tim Williams (U.S. Air Force).

New Opportunities in Artificial Intelligence

Mr. Arnold is a subject-matter expert at the Pentagon working in the areas of trusted artificial intelligence (AI) and autonomy. (He also presented at the April 24–25 Town Hall; see Chapter 3.) "We do not have a diverse workforce moving forward," he stated, and addressing this gap is one area in which he is working. He commented that the U.S. Supreme Court decision against affirmative action will stymie some pathways, but there are ways to move forward to increase diversity.

The future operational environment at DOD will need AI and autonomy, he stressed. "We need students who understand the adversary and are well trained in key areas," he said. It is important to identify promising students and support them. When he speaks with university students, faculty, and administrators, he calls attention to the need for collaboration and partnerships. Some schools have less infrastructure than others, but all are needed to address national needs. The AI opportunities for trained students include calibration of trust, information protection, explainability and interpretability, performance in the field, and robustness to adversarial attacks. He called attention to the Science, Mathematics, and Research for Transformation (SMART) and other DOD scholarship and fellowship opportunities to support students in their studies.[1]

Community College to 4-Year Transitions at George Mason University

Dr. Hilker-Balkissoon described several programs at George Mason University to address systemic and student inequities in science, technology, engineering, and mathematics (STEM) transfer for community college students, which she said are an overlooked population for STEM-sector readiness. She noted GMU is the largest public research university and the largest producer of STEM talent in Virginia. It is also ranked seventh nationally in terms of its diversity.

According to Dr. Hilker-Balkissoon, the value proposition to invest in the 2-to-4-year transfer pipeline stems from the fact that more than 40 percent of U.S. undergraduates matriculate in community colleges, a disproportionate number of whom are from underserved and minoritized communities. Most students are place based and are more likely to stay in the region to work. She noted the need for 2- and 4-year institutions to cross-align curricula to reduce credit loss when students transfer.

ADVANCE is GMU's guided pathways program launched in 2018. It serves more than 3,600 students, 45 percent of whom are in STEM fields. Retention is very strong at about 83 percent (versus the national average of 61 percent). In addition to minimizing credit loss, ADVANCE provides ways for community college students to engage in research. The Mason Science Transfer Equity and Success Initiative was launched in 2018 to supplement and complement ADVANCE. It was based on a needs assessment that identified barriers to transfer students from accessing research opportunities at an equitable level compared with direct-entry students. A design thinking approach focuses on developing social, cultural, and career capital.

Barriers identified were that community college students are not getting information about research opportunities or the value of research to their careers. Many students had only inaccurate media representations of

[1] For more information on SMART, see https://dodstem.us/participate/smart/.

potential STEM careers. Only 11 percent of incoming transfer students said they planned to engage in research in their first semester. Access, equity, and inclusion barriers included how research opportunities were offered to students, as well as some faculty members' inaccurate perceptions about the students' academic preparation. In addition, many opportunities are designed for traditional students who are not working, and these opportunities are not accessible to many nontraditional students.

Both student-focused interventions and systemic interventions were developed. The student interventions included building a community and offering both outreach and inreach supports to ensure students are STEM career-ready.[2] Systemic interventions take longer but are needed, she continued. One of the most impactful was to include transfer students within the school's JEDI (justice, equity, diversity, and inclusion) goals. That opened up institutional support and funding, such as training of community college advisors.

Focusing on several of the interventions, the Scientific Community of Transfer Researchers (SCTR) program offers a nonresidential learning community for cohorts of students in the fall and spring. The overall goal is to enhance career readiness by leveraging undergraduate research. After learning about the research process in an initial course, students are ready for mentored research in the coming semesters. The early outcomes have been very successful in accessing opportunities, she said. The next phase, the Research and Interdisciplinary STEM Experiences (RISE) Scholars Program, builds on lessons learned from SCTR, Dr. Hilker-Balkissoon explained. Students learn data visualization and other research skills, then participate in research and internship experiences. They receive stipends and scholarships to participate, and some hybrid and virtual experiences are offered to ensure all students have access.

Workforce Pipeline for DEVCOM

Dr. Mello discussed a model developed through the National Defense Education Program to enhance the workforce pipeline for DEVCOM and DOD overall, with a focus on undergraduate and graduate students. The funding is designed to develop an agile workforce in synthetic biology across a wide partnership with many Minority-Serving Institutions (MSIs), as well as with military and veteran partners. A team is composed of Army

[2] For more information, see https://science.gmu.edu/transfer.

scientists and engineers, students, and faculty to help create awareness of DOD opportunities. Dr. Mello said the teams are co-creating materials in synthetic biology and educating partners about DOD's science and technology (S&T) challenges and how to get involved (see Figure 7-1).

Students, led by faculty, work with defense scientists to research a relevant area of synthetic biology. A Virtual Distributed Student Network has been developed to explore career opportunities in the field and, more generally, to learn to develop and appreciate the power of a professional network and other career-building skills. A variety of activities are taking place aligned with end-of-program goals. The first year of the program recently concluded.

University Affiliated Research Center at Howard University

Mr. Williams highlighted the Tactical Autonomy University Affiliated Research Center (UARC) led by Howard University and involving eight additional Historically Black Colleges and Universities (HBCUs) in a consortium, which was mentioned throughout the town halls. The consortium members have different Carnegie classifications (Carnegie Classification system) and other characteristics related to research. He noted several technical lines of effort, as well as the thrusts and objectives related to K–12 outreach, postsecondary students and faculty, and support for R2 institutions to transition to R1.

According to Mr. Williams, lessons learned to date are that, first, many universities and students are not aware of DOD opportunities, other than of people in uniform. Second, exposure is limited. Third, teaching loads for faculty are heavy. Fourth, the institutions' Offices of Sponsored Research are small, especially to manage contract requirements. Solutions are being identified, he added. A positive aspect is the number of diverse U.S. citizens in STEM fields at HBCUs is higher than at Predominantly White Institutions, or PWIs, and these institutions can provide cleared personnel to DOD and other employers.

Discussion

Discussing how to dispel the myth that DOD research only involves weapon development, Dr. Mello suggested greater education and exposure to existing S&T portfolios in both fundamental and applied research. Dr. Hilker-Balkissoon suggested reaching out to career centers, advising teams,

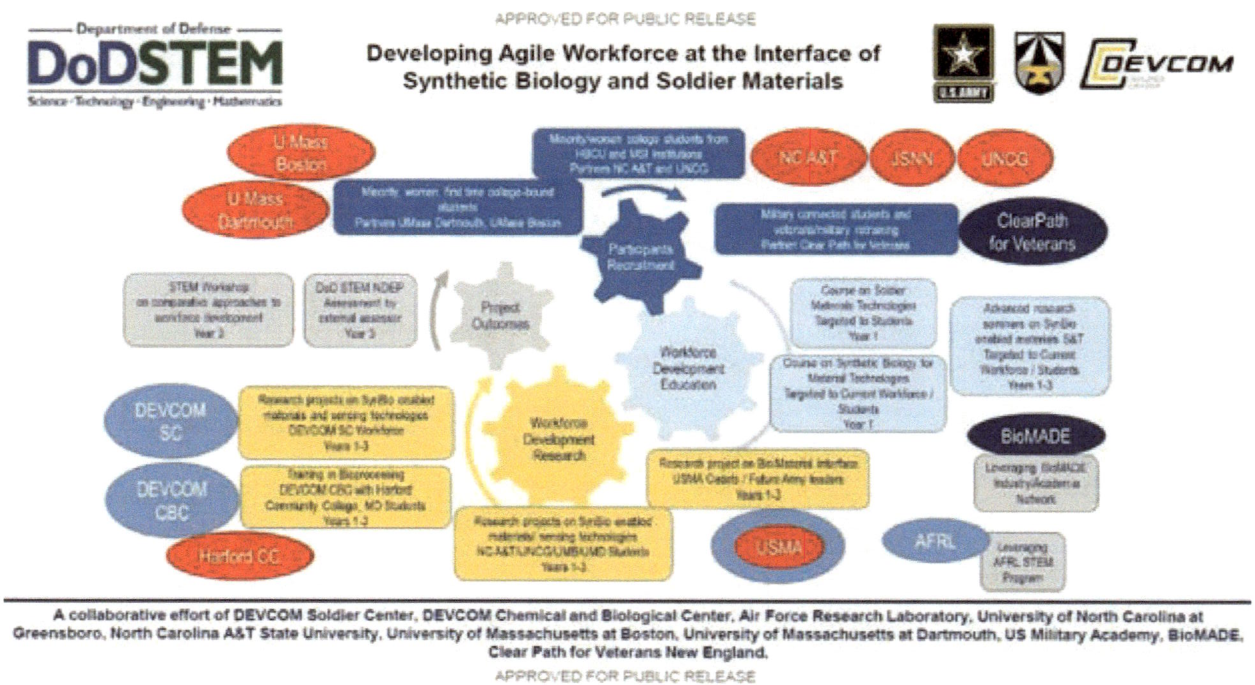

FIGURE 7-1 Developing agile workforce at the interface of synthetic biology and soldier materials.
SOURCE: Christine Mello, Town Hall Presentation, June 29, 2023.

and others who can provide information to students and faculty. This could expand the reach akin to a train-the-trainer model, she suggested.

CHALLENGES AND OPPORTUNITIES FOR RESEARCHERS AND PERSONNEL ENGAGING IN FEDERALLY FUNDED RESEARCH

In introducing the next panel, Oscar Barton, Jr., Ph.D., P.E. (Morgan State University), noted the continuing references throughout the workshop to the role of faculty in building the research enterprise, as well as different challenges and opportunities for faculty at different career levels. Jill Keith, Ph.D. (Winston-Salem State University [WSSU]), Michael Groves, Ph.D. (California State University, Fullerton [CSUF]), Abraham Wolcott, Ph.D. (San José State University [SJSU]), and Saleh Zein-Sabatto, Ph.D. (Tennessee State University [TSU]), provided their perspectives.

Winston-Salem State University

Dr. Keith introduced Winston-Salem State University and pointed to the challenge of time in order for faculty to stay on top of research. Faculty at HBCUs have heavy teaching, committee, and service responsibilities. K–12 STEM outreach and student advising also take time. WSSU has a small but growing Office of Sponsored Programs, and the university's strategic plan sets a goal to move to R2. As she commented, funding follows a strategic plan.

Student success is the top priority at WSSU. High-impact practices include providing opportunities for student research and reducing student debt. Thus, research programs pay students a competitive salary ($15–$20 hourly) so they do not have to take other types of jobs out of economic necessity. Through research opportunities, they gain an appreciation of the benefits of scientific research and interdisciplinary partnerships.

WSSU is located next to Wake Forest School of Medicine, which has resulted in a number of partnerships and three joint grants for research and faculty development. Other joint proposals have been submitted, and she underscored the benefits of working with other institutions. An associate provost has been hired to drive the institution to R2 status. WSSU obtained its first patent and is looking at other patents and spin-off projects. However, without sufficient staff, faculty have to do the administrative work themselves, Dr. Keith said.

California State University, Fullerton

Dr. Groves shared data about the campuses that compose California State University and reminded participants about the state's higher education structure in which CSU campuses emphasize teaching and the University of California (UC) campuses prioritize research. Within this structure, Dr. Groves shared how the CSUF Department of Chemistry and Biochemistry exposes students to research through a capstone requirement that most students fulfill by doing research with a faculty principal investigator in a lab. Over the last 5 years, as a result of this requirement, 293 undergraduates presented at scientific meetings and 153 students were co-authors on peer-reviewed publications. The goal is to show students that they can be part of the scientific community and get involved in the research process, he said. Many go on to graduate STEM work.

Dr. Groves highlighted his own research on physical hole deficits, including using AI and machine learning, with areas of interest to DOD that include diamond surface properties for high-powered electronics. He explained that a DOD research scientist read about his work and reached out to him as a faculty member at an MSI, offering opportunities for both students and faculty.

To Dr. Groves, a challenge is that the administration does not prioritize research excellence or capacity among its strategic goals. While research is framed as a high-impact practice and research achievements are lauded, he said there is no investment in developing research agendas. Noting he was contacted by the DOD scientist somewhat by chance, he said it is difficult to learn about opportunities proactively. To him, the research administration is set up to manage, rather than enable, faculty.

As an opportunity, he said CSUF can help DOD develop the pipeline for underrepresented students to reach the "missing millions." He noted that he continues to look for opportunities for students especially in the Southern California region.

San José State University

Workshop committee member Dr. Wolcott spoke about his research program at San José State University, another CSU campus. He noted he could give his talk a technical title about the scientific focus or title it "Experience and Wisdom Performing High-Quality Research with Undergraduates While Remaining Rational." He highlighted his areas of research focus and education and career pathway. He quoted Freeman Dyson, who said, "New directions in science are launched by new tools much more often than new concepts." A tool-driven revolution is occurring now with AI, machine learning, and materials-related research. He also noted new methods and modalities will expand the DOD ecosystem.

His research laboratory usually has 15 to 20 students in several research thrusts. The goal is a robust architecture to maintain research programs without interruption. Dr. Wolcott said his experience as an undergraduate and graduate student at UC Santa Cruz showed how to take advantage of the rich research ecosystem in the Bay Area. Dr. Wolcott has mentored more than 60 students, and 10 have gone to Ph.D. studies, all from underrepresented groups. He has collaborated with SJSU's Black Leadership and Opportunities Center to recruit Black student researchers into the lab, which he said could be a model throughout the Cal State system, and highlighted some of the lab's accomplishments. He noted SJSU provides faculty release time, which he stressed is important to free up time for research, management, publishing, and other tasks. Donated instrumentation is an important resource. "You have to be open and talkative and take advantage of the opportunities," he said.

Challenges to the research enterprise at SJSU include limited large capital instrumentation, poor infrastructure quality, and the need to maintain a large group of student researchers to meet the critical lab knowledge threshold for continuity. Faculty must be aware that students have many external pressures—such as violence, fear of deportation, and other issues. As a faculty member, he said it is difficult to find the time to publish because of teaching, research, and administration responsibilities, so there is a constant hustle. As a positive development, SJSU has a new science building, and his lab will have space in it.

Dr. Wolcott offered recommendations for DOD and SJSU. For DOD, he recommended requiring universities to acknowledge and write articles about awarded faculty; posting changes in HBCU/Minority Institution award criteria a year in advance so accommodations to the changes can be made; disclosing changes in allowable costs; assigning specific program managers to enhance communication; and creating DOD-based training programs similar to the National Institutes of Health's (NIH) Maximizing Access to Research Careers (MARC) and RISE programs.[3]

---

[3] For more information on MARC, see https://nigms.nih.gov/training/MARC/Pages/USTARAwards.aspx. For more information on RISE, see https://nigms.nih.gov/training/RISE.

For SJSU, he recommended acknowledgment of successful research faculty, hiring technical staff to maintain and aid research, reducing non-technical administrative hires, reducing the administrative burden on faculty by pooling resources, maintaining infrastructure, asking research faculty what they need to succeed, providing meritorious salary, and hiring more Black and Hispanic STEM faculty.

Tennessee State University

Dr. Zein-Sabatto teaches; conducts research funded by the National Science Foundation (NSF), NASA, and DOD; and serves as a department chair in the College of Engineering at Tennessee State University. TSU, located in Nashville, has about 9,000 students, 68 percent of whom are African American, and the College of Engineering has about 900 students. (See also presentations from TSU in Chapter 6.) A goal for the university is to transition to R1 in the next 5 to 10 years. "It's all about students," he stressed, as a focus for TSU and other HBCUs and MSIs. Many students have gone on to graduate education or to work in federal agencies.

Dr. Zein-Sabatto identified several challenges in common with other HBCUs and MSIs, including high teaching loads, little support staff for proposal development, and the need to attract high-quality graduate students. Much of the focus in graduate recruitment is within the institution by encouraging current undergraduate and master's students to consider doctoral study at TSU. That helps students, faculty researchers, and the institution. Most engineering faculty at TSU are international. They are excellent faculty members, but they cannot pursue some research because of their citizenship status. Overall, the teaching load prevents faculty from networking, which limits their collaborative research and ability to pursue new areas. Junior faculty in particular struggle with how to apportion their time. He suggested targeting these faculty and funding them to attend workshops, since they are the faculty of the future.

Discussion

Dr. Barton asked presenters to envision what ideal research administration support would look like. Dr. Groves said a partner who would help faculty solve challenges. For example, there is no consistency about how to pay students at his institution. A participant commented that there is no standardization across institutions about compensating students and providing health benefits, but there are tax implications about which students may be unaware, especially students with families. As another ideal practice, Dr. Zein-Sabatto suggested staff support to take care of budgeting and other documentation needed for proposals, and when grants are awarded, to submit invoices in a timely manner. Dr. Wolcott stressed the need for technically trained staff. He urged a recalibration of budgets to fund these types of positions as a human capital issue.

Related to high teaching loads, Dr. Zein-Sabatto said TSU has a policy that sets a minimum of teaching 12 credits per semester. The policy is being rethought, and one idea is to have research-oriented and teaching-oriented faculty categories. Tenure policies would have to be revised, however, as there are minimum teaching loads to get tenure. Dr. Keith said negotiations for course release with department chairs can be undertaken at WSSU, but it depends on the chair. The availability of adjunct faculty factors into the decision. Dr. Groves said the capstone requirement at CSUF allows for some teaching relief.

Mentorship and networking can play a big role, Dr. Barton observed. Dr. Wolcott concurred and said his own mentorship journey began when he was an undergraduate, including learning the mindset to always look for new opportunities. He has passed that on to his own students. Dr. Zein-Sabatto said one way he mentors junior faculty is to include them in proposals as co-principal investigators in their first or second year on campus. They are encouraged to take the lead in follow-up proposals.

FEDERAL CAPACITY PROGRAMS FOR FACULTY AND TRAINEE SUPPORT

As noted throughout the town halls, federal agencies provide a range of supports to graduate, postdoctoral, and early-career researchers, as well as offer professional development. In the last panel, committee member Keith McGee, Ph.D. (Alcorn State University), moderated a session with Narcrisha Norman, Ph.D. (NSF), Sailaja Koduri, Ph.D. (NIH), and LaRico Treadwell, Ph.D. (Sandia National Laboratories), for what he termed a 360-degree perspective of the research ecosystem, from support of graduate students to postdocs to early- and mid-career faculty.

National Science Foundation

Dr. Norman spoke about the National Science Foundation's Graduate Research Fellowship Program (GRFP), which she said is one of NSF's oldest and largest fellowship programs.[4] Located within the Directorate of STEM Education, GRFP offers 3 years of financial support over a 5-year fellowship period, and it is open to individuals pursuing research-based master's and doctoral degrees in eligible fields. About 12,000 applications are received per round, about 2,000 offers made, and about 500 institutions are represented. She stressed the value to applicants to submit early. A decision tree and format compliance check are helpful resources on the GRFP website, she added. Dr. Norman explained other aspects of the application package, eligibility criteria, and timeline. A comprehensive review is conducted to evaluate an application's intellectual merit (how important the proposed activity is to advancing knowledge within its own field or across different fields) and broader impact (how well the proposed activity benefits society or advances desired social outcomes), based on National Science Board Merit Review Criteria. Applicants are evaluated based on their demonstrated potential for significant achievements in STEM, using a comprehensive holistic approach and balanced consideration of all components of the application.

National Institutes of Health

Dr. Koduri discussed several graduate and early-faculty efforts within the National Institute of General Medical Sciences (NIGMS) and other institutes and centers at the National Institutes of Health to promote diversity, along with relevant identifying numbers to access further information.

The Maximizing Opportunities for Scientific and Academic Independent Careers (MOSAIC) Program was designed to promote diversity by facilitating the timely transition of promising postdoctoral researchers from diverse backgrounds from their mentored positions to independent, tenure-track or equally research-intensive faculty positions. It consists of support to the candidates (K99/R00, PAR-21-271) and additional mentoring, networking, and career development through research education centers at scientific societies (UE5, PAR-21-277).

NIGMS Technology Development Programs support the earliest stages of technology development, establishing feasibility/proof of concept and prototype validations (R01, PAR-22-127; R21, PAR-22-126).

[4] For more information, see https://nsfgrfp.org/ and www.nsf.gov/grfp.

Research Enhancement Awards support small-scale research projects at educational institutions that provide baccalaureate or advanced degrees for a significant number of the nation's research scientists but that have not been major recipients of NIH support (institutions that have received less than $6 million per year from NIH in 4 of the last 7 years). NIGMS participates in the Academic Research Enhancement Award (PAR-21-155) within NIH's R15 larger award program.

To promote research capacity building at institutions with lower NIH support and at least 25 percent of enrollment supported by Pell Grants, the SuRE (Support for Research Excellence) Program has two types of awards (R16, PAR-21-173 and PAR-21-169) for full-time faculty investigators.

The NIGMS Maximizing Investigators' Research Award (MIRA) began in 2016 to allow early (PAR-23-145) and more established and new (PAR-22-180) investigators to spend more time on research and mentoring to enhance their ability to move into research. It is designed to provide flexible and stable funding to the investigators. She described the criteria and application process in greater detail. She noted that by FY 2022, a significant number of Early Stage Investigator, or ESI, grants were MIRA awards. One of NIGMS's strategic goals is to have 60 percent of its R01-equivalent pool to be MIRAs by 2025. She called attention to NIGMS's feedback loop blog posts for further information.[5]

Sandia National Laboratories

Dr. Treadwell is the technical research liaison to a program that began at Sandia National Laboratories 3 years ago called the Securing Top Academic Research and Talent at Historically Black Colleges and Universities Program (START HBCU). He noted the value to date and plans to expand it.

START HBCU began with a review of the demographics of the lab workforce, which is about 2.2 percent African American/Black. The analysis showed that most African American candidates come from partner schools, but only three of Sandia's existing partners were HBCUs. Reaching beyond the existing partnership schools, START HBCU was designed to address the lab's responsibility as a Federally Funded Research and Development

[5] For more information, see https://loop.nigms.nih.gov.

Corporation, its contractual obligations, and its corporate goals and objectives to diversify the workforce.[6]

Dr. Treadwell explained further analysis of HBCUs was undertaken to look at such criteria as publication alignment with Sandia areas of research and NSF data. A rubric was developed to evaluate which HBCUs could form a START HBCU pilot. Immediate, near-term, and long-term goals were set up in recruiting, program partnerships, research, and partnership development. Academic programs include a faculty loan program, diversity partnership, university partnership network, and postdoctoral program office. He noted the list of institutions is constantly evolving and changing, and he welcomed new participants with the goal to grow a diverse research talent pipeline.

Dr. Treadwell summarized START HBCU's programmatic and technical accomplishments and upcoming milestones. A START HBCU Intern Institute has involved 30 students. Opportunities to collaborate with Sandia include a Critical Skills Program for students, internships, fellowships, research collaborations, letters of support, mentorship, and a two-way faculty loan program.

Discussion

Dr. Norman noted a number of other NSF programs are designed to reach students at HBCUs, Hispanic-Serving Institutions (HSIs), and Tribal Colleges and Universities (TCUs), in addition to GRFP. (See Chapters 3 and 5 for several such programs.) Dr. Koduri explained the MOSAIC program at NIH is for postdoctoral students within their first 5 years. One aspect of the program is to help them negotiate when they do attain an independent position to ensure a successful transition. She noted NIGMS also has some programs for high school and undergraduate students.[7]

Faculty release time has been a frequent topic throughout the town halls, Dr. McGee pointed out. A challenge for rural or other marginalized campuses is to find replacement faculty if they do get release time. Dr. Treadwell said the faculty loan program envisioned through START HBCU may be a model. Many Sandia researchers want to teach and, through the loan program, they can travel or teach virtually in a win-win situation with

[6] For more information, see www.sandia.gov/about/.

[7] For more information, see https://nigms.nih.gov/research-training/programs/high-school-and-undergraduate.

institutions seeking faculty release arrangements. He and other Sandia staff try to build connections with faculty. He also noted that Sandia is discussing how to work with TCUs.

CONCLUDING DISCUSSION

The town hall ended with a discussion among committee members and participants about some of the points raised throughout the town hall series about capacity building, true partnerships, and federal programs to support research ecosystems at institutions.

Building Capacity

Dr. Barton noted that in the conversation to identify barriers to build DOD research at MSIs, it was clear that the barriers at different institutions are not the same. Some relate to infrastructure, while others stem from lack of recognition of what the institutions are already doing and have to offer. Large institutions have the resources to continue growing but face other challenges. To build capacity, he continued, faculty are the linchpin to success, and it is important to reimagine what faculty workloads encompass, including research, teaching, and service expectations. If an institution sees research as a priority, policies must align with this. It is incumbent on leadership to enhance what the expectations of a vibrant research culture look like and then take actions and provide resources based on this vision. Many institutions are building out their infrastructure and need initial investments from DOD, foundations, and others. Several valuable programs were discussed that can help jumpstart this process, he pointed out. He also pointed to programs that support students from the undergraduate level through their terminal degree that could be aligned with the missions of DOD labs and other initiatives.

Dr. McGee reflected on the perceptions on campuses about the needs of faculty researchers. He urged greater communication so that faculty and administrators understand each other's needs and pressure points. When working with partners at DOD and others in the federal government, it is also important to build trust between institutions and agencies.

Andrea Christelle, Ph.D. (Diné College), noted that some institutions are already conducting research and it is a matter of expanding their programs. In contrast, TCUs were founded with the mission to allow tribal communities to have a higher education experience close to home and to strengthen language preservation. Developing a research program is new, and many are starting from zero. Building up something that exists and starting something anew present two different considerations for capacity building, she observed.

Dr. Barton pointed out in discussing research capacity, most MSIs focus on grants, but contracts present an opportunity to elevate or enhance the research at an institution. Dr. McGee said building capacity should involve ensuring that more than one person understands a process because if that person leaves, they exit with institutional knowledge.

Helen Turner, Ph.D. (Chaminade University of Honolulu), commented that capacity building has institutional and personal aspects. Changing the faculty's way of thinking about their roles is not easy. Many consider their teaching as important as research, she observed. Administrators need to reskill, upskill, and support existing faculty who want to do research, but also hire for the research mission going forward. Looking ahead 5 years, she envisioned a structure at Chaminade and other small institutions with research-empowered faculty while, in parallel, moving current faculty along the research continuum.

Dr. Wolcott reflected that geography and space are a factor across institutions and present unique challenges. For example, he said, building research capacity is different across Cal State campuses, TCUs, HSIs in urban environments, and other settings. For this reason, he said, DOD programs have to be flexible. He urged wording in funding announcements that allow teams to be creative at their institutions and allow for innovation. Institutions must identify their challenges, whether related to infrastructure, teaching loads, geographic location, or other considerations, he added.

Dr. Groves stressed the lens of student development and building a pipeline for DOD. The human capital of students could be a unifying focus, he suggested. Dr. Wolcott agreed but said it should be coupled with faculty development. Without faculty maintaining research and staying at institutions long term, the impact on students will be minimized. Dr. McGee agreed that student development and faculty development must occur in tandem. Dr. Christelle added the need for development and investment in research administration to sustain the effort.

Dr. Turner said that when Chaminade University became part of the Howard Hughes Medical Institute's (HHMI's) Inclusive Excellence Program, what resonated was HHMI's emphasis not to "fix students," but instead to fix systems. That narrative applies here, she posited. It is important to change the perception to show that research at small institutions is meaningful to the nation's STEM landscape and should be a national priority. Dr. Wolcott suggested one strategy is for institutions to spotlight faculty accomplishments.

True Partnerships

Chad Womack, Ph.D. (United Negro College Fund [UNCF]), reflected on conversations about true partnerships, to include agencies, larger institutions, UARCS, and peer-to-peer partnerships. A common denominator is to make sure these partnerships are win-win. Drilling down, he asked, what does that mean? He suggested making sure that HBCUs and MSIs are not on the losing end of resources and that they are left better off at the end and not worse. Part of that is retention of faculty, referring to examples where HBCU faculty were recruited to the larger institution in a partnership.

The recently launched Applied Research Institute for Applied Mathematics and other models are built on the notion that there are resources and assets in that HBCU community that can be leveraged, he said.[8] It is important to be intentional about how to network research faculty to allow them to grow, such as through joint and adjunct appointments, and to incentivize institutions to participate. Other issues that come into play include intellectual property, tech transfer, and commercialization in order for institutions to capture the value of the research. He urged capacity building around commercialization to go after bigger opportunities.

Dr. Barton said partnerships require "truth in advertising" so that relationships are built that are valued and trusted. Dr. Christelle reflected on situations in which TCUs enter into partnerships with R1s, but they do not benefit from commercialization. A tech transfer office, even a small business development office, at a TCU can show what is possible to students. Dr. McGee commented that land created wealth in the past, but new technology creates wealth today. It is important that smaller institutions are part of the conversation.

Dr. Barton asked about the model of a mentorship between a small and a larger institution. Dr. Christelle said Diné College has a strong relationship with the University of Arizona, which has provided valuable technical

[8] For more information, see https://uncf.org/news/uncf-and-google-are-paving-the-path-forward-to-increase-opportunities-for-hbcu-students-in-tech-fields-with-additional-2m-investment.

assistance. Yet, the two institutions are vastly different, and she stressed the value of a TCU consortium to support one another.

Dr. Turner commented on the importance of personal relationships in learning about federal funding opportunities, perhaps from a meeting at a conference or other encounter. Figuring out how to take the element of chance out of these connections is an important question, she said. Getting everyone on board with a collective impact framework can decrease tokenism of involving a smaller or less resourced institution. It would help if pathways to funding for smaller institutions were more formalized, she suggested.

Federal Opportunities

Reflecting on federal opportunities, Dr. McGee commented that each workshop has provided examples of stellar programs. It is important for these programs to be intentional and deliberate so that all institutions benefit, he said. He suggested that consortia of TCUs, HBCUs, HSIs, and other institutions work with each other, as well as groups like UNCF and the Thurgood Marshall Fund, to have a bigger role in federal capacity-building decisions. Dr. Womack agreed on the impact of "go-together strategies." Across the landscape, centers and/or individual faculty are doing great work that could be leveraged. He suggested networks in such a way that institutions are not going after individual NSF grants but larger funding opportunities together. He also noted contract opportunities at DOD and in the private sector that cannot be achieved without working together.

Dr. McGee asked about building the management and legal infrastructure to take advantage of these opportunities. Dr. Barton noted that industry and agencies have different needs and timelines. Dr. Wolcott commented that federal opportunities, particularly contracts, are difficult to identify and pursue for individual faculty members. Dr. Barton said leadership must be aware and engaged to facilitate the pursuit of contracts. Dr. McGee said a grant tends to be the brainchild of a specific faculty member, but a contract, in general, is aligned with an agency's mission. If the expertise is on campus, the institution can take advantage of these opportunities, but someone on campus must be looking out for them. Federal partnerships are critical to the survival and ability to train students for the next-generation workforce. Being able to work with federal partners is very important. Having transparent conversations can lead to a greater understanding of what is needed, he asserted.

Dr. Barton closed this town hall by thanking panelists, committee members, staff, and others for coming to the table. He thanked DOD for the opportunity to put institutions in a place where they can be engaged.

Appendix A

Town Hall Agendas

Defense Research Capacity at HBCUs, TCUs, HSIs, and ANNHSIs: Town Hall on Capacity Development (April 24 and 25, 2023): Transformational and Transactional Culture Shifts (Hybrid)

MONDAY, APRIL 24, 2023
Purpose

- Highlight barriers that dissuade capacity-building activities at MIs.
- Investigate faculty workload policies.
- Elucidate strategies for research portfolio diversification.
- Address the threshold for infrastructure investments.

10:00 – 10:10 Opening Remarks
Oscar Barton, Jr., Ph.D., P.E., Committee Chair

10:10 – 12:00 Barriers to Building Defense-Related Research Capacity
The first session of day 1 will include a series of panels with representatives across Minority Institution designations (HBCUs, TCU, HSIs, etc.) to discuss the challenges their institutions and like institutions face when developing defense-related capacity.

Panel 1 – HBCUs
Moderator: **Oscar Barton, Jr., Ph.D., P.E.** – Morgan State University

Panelists:
John M. Anderson, Ph.D. – Howard University
Farin Kamangar, M.D., Ph.D. – Morgan State University

Panel 2 – TCUs
Moderator: **Abraham Wolcott, Ph.D.** – San José State University

Panelists:
Andrea Christelle, Ph.D. – Diné College
Al Kuslikis – American Indian Higher Education Consortium
Emily Biggane, Ph.D. – United Tribes Technical College

Panel 3 – HSIs
Moderator: **Abraham Wolcott, Ph.D.** – San José State University

Panelists:
Karen Butler, Ph.D. – Texas A&M University
Frank A. Gomez, Ph.D. – Cal State System
Folarin Erogbogbo, Ph.D. – San José State University

Panel 4 –ANNHSI
Moderator: **Abraham Wolcott, Ph.D.** – San José State University

Panelists:
Helen Turner, Ph.D. – Chaminade University of Honolulu
Aaron Dotson, Ph.D. – University of Alaska Anchorage
Michele Yatchmeneff, Ph.D. – University of Alaska Anchorage

12:00 – 12:15 Break

12:15 – 1:20 Reimagining Faculty Workload Policies
The session will highlight best practices used by a diverse suite of institutions to provide novel opportunities for administrators at MIs to incorporate that offer room for faculty to participate in research and better balance teaching loads.

Moderator: **Oscar Barton, Jr., Ph.D., P.E.** – Morgan State University

Panelists:
Mark Ginsberg, Ph.D. – George Mason University
John Crockett, Ph.D. – San Diego State University

1:20 – 1:30 Break

1:30 – 2:45 Culture and Leadership Models to Facilitate Research Capacity Building
The last session of the day will explore institutions that have successfully shifted to be more responsive to the Department of Defense's research priorities through institutional culture shifts and leadership models. Panelists will outline both institutional policies and procedures and DOD programs and policies that have facilitated a more robust research enterprise within their institutions.

Moderator: **Abigail S. Newsome, Ph.D.** – Mississippi Valley State University

Panelists:
Jagannathan Sankar, Ph.D. – North Carolina A&T University
Twyla Baker, Ph.D. – Nueta Hidatsa Sahnish College

2:45 – 3:00 Closing Remarks and Recapitulation of Day 1

END OF DAY 1

TUESDAY, APRIL 25, 2023

10:00 – 11:30 Developing a Diverse Funding Portfolio
The first session of day 2 will highlight the diversity in funding opportunities at the Department of Defense (grants, contracts, etc.) and strategies that institutions have successfully adopted to facilitate the acquisition of diverse funding streams from the DOD.

Moderator: **Oscar Barton, Jr., Ph.D., P.E.** – Morgan State University

Panelist:
Kamal Khayat, Ph.D. – Missouri University of Science and Technology

11:30 – 12:30 Addressing the Critical Threshold for Infrastructure Investments
A panel of experts and stakeholders will elucidate the necessary investments in infrastructure for adequate participation in the Department of Defense's research portfolio. Topics of discussion will include an investigation of critical thresholds, funding opportunities for infrastructure development, and strategies for institutions and the DOD to consider toward support for research infrastructure.

Moderator: **Chad Womack, Ph.D.** – United Negro College Fund

Panelists:
Shannon Arnold, M.Eng., M.S. – GBL Systems Corporation
Victor McCrary, Ph.D. – University of the District of Columbia
Jaret C. Riddick, Ph.D. – Center for Security and Emerging Technology

12:30 – 1:30 Break

1:30 – 2:30 Federal Capacity Building Programs
The final session of day 2 will spotlight federal programs that address research capacity-building needs through funding opportunities and other intervention methods.

Moderator: **Keith A. McGee, Ph.D.** – Alcorn State University

Panelists:
Natalia Melcer – Department of Energy, Office of Science
Dina Stroud, Ph.D. – National Science Foundation, GRANTED program

2:30 – 3:00 Recapitulation of Day 1 and Day 2 Strategies and Federal Programs

Closing Remarks

MEETING ADJOURNS

Building Defense Research Capacity at HBCUs, TCUs, HSIs, and ANNHSIs: Town Hall on True Partnerships (May 22 and 23, 2023)
Albuquerque, NM (Hybrid)

MONDAY, MAY 22, 2023 (MST)
Purpose

- Provide an overview of the defense R&D environment.
- Illustrate strategies for articulating the value proposition for partnership development.
- Outline defense industry criteria for developing partnerships with academic institutions.
- Spotlight historic and current models for the development of synergistic partnerships

10:20 – 10:30 Opening Remarks

10:30 – 11:30 Igniting the Defense Research Ecosystem
The panelist for the first session will provide an overview of the stakeholders relevant to a high-functioning defense research environment that includes higher education institutions, the Department of Defense, industry, and others. Additionally, the session will spotlight partnerships that have led to productive activities in research and development and the matriculation of students into careers within the defense R&D environment.

Moderator: **Melvin Greer, Ph.D.** – Intel Corporation

Panelists:
Victor McCrary, Ph.D. – University of the District of Columbia
Santosh Devasia, Ph.D. – University of Washington
Thomas Tubon, Ph.D. – BioMADE

11:30 – 11:50 Break

11:50 – 12:50 Articulating the Value Proposition for Equitable Partnerships
The second session will highlight strategies for relationship building and partnership outreach used by industry and academic institutions to socialize scientific research priorities and capabilities to facilitate mutualistic partnerships.

Moderator: **Oscar Barton, Ph.D.** – Morgan State University

Panelists:
Eric Adolphe, Esq. – Forward Edge-AI, Inc.
Christina "Chris" Deckard – Office of the Under Secretary of Defense, Biotechnology
Robert St. Amant, Ph.D. – DEVCOM Army Research Laboratory

12:50 – 1:10 Break

1:10 – 2:10 Models for Synergistic Partnerships
The third session will consist of a panel of university-industry-government partnerships that exhibit equitable relationships between organizations. Representatives from highlighted partnerships will provide best practices and recommendations for how academic institutions, industry, and the DOD can nurture true partnerships through policies and programs.

Moderator: **Bryn Adams, Ph.D.** – DEVCOM Army Research Laboratory

Panelists:
Kelly Freidenfelds, Ph.D. – Princeton-HBCU Alliance for Collaborative Research
Robert Shepard, Ph.D. – The Shepard Institute LLC
Aaron Wecksler, Ph.D. – Genentech

2:10 – 2:30 Closing Remarks and Recapitulation of Day 1

END OF DAY 1

TUESDAY, MAY 23, 2023 (MST)

10:00 – 11:30 Institutional Challenges to Developing Partnerships
The fourth session of the workshop will provide insight into the obstacles encountered by HBCUs, TCUs, smaller HSIs, and ANNHSIs. A panel of representatives from each institution type will provide insight into the complications, limitations, and potential investment areas for the DOD to explore.

Moderator: **Abigail S. Newsome, Ph.D.** – Mississippi Valley State University

Panelists:
Ganesh C. Bora, Ph.D. – Fayetteville State University
Elmer Guy, Ph.D. – Navajo Technical University
Teresa Orok, Ph.D. – Alabama A&M University
Sheryl H. Ehrman, Ph.D., P.E. – San José State University

11:30 – 11:40 Break

11:40 – 12:20 Applied Research Institute for Mathematics and Computational Sciences
Chad Womack, Ph.D. – United Negro College Fund

12:20 – 12:30 Break

12:30 – 1:30 Federal Partnership Programs
The final panel will spotlight federal agency programs that have successfully facilitated the development of equitable partnerships between institutions (like and unlike) and industry. Panelists will be directed to outline how those programs were created and maintained and how outcome tracking is facilitated.

Moderator: **Keith McGee, Ph.D.** – Alcorn State University

Panelists:
Jesus V. Soriano Molla, Ph.D. – National Science Foundation
Terrence Mosley, M.S. – Department of Energy

1:30 – 2:00 Recapitulation of Day 1 and Day 2 Strategies and Federal Programs

Closing Remarks

MEETING ADJOURNS

Building Defense Research Capacity at HBCUs, TCUs, HSIs, and ANNHSIs: Final Town Hall (June 28 and 29, 2023)
Chicago, IL (Hybrid)

WEDNESDAY, JUNE 28, 2023 (CST)

Purpose

- Evaluate the components necessary to elevate an institution's research activity.
- Highlight research faculty and personnel support structures.
- Investigate recruitment strategies for research-centered faculty.
- Revisit the topics and discussions included throughout the series.

9:00 – 9:05 Opening Remarks

Moderator: **Oscar Barton, Ph.D.**, Morgan State University – Chair of the Workshop Committee on Building Defense Research Capacity at Historically Black Colleges and Universities and Other Minority Institutions

9:05 – 10:00 Transitioning from Low to High Research Activity
The first session of day one will discuss the actions necessary for institutions with historically low to no research activity to transition to high/very high research output successfully. Spotlighted institutions will illustrate the strategies used to ramp up their research activities and academic standing toward securing more federal funding and expanding their research capabilities.

Moderator: **Tom Tubon, Ph.D.** – BioMADE

Panelists:
Rosemarie Wesson, Ph.D. – CUNY City College
Gillian Wilson, Ph.D. – University of California, Merced

10:00 – 11:00 Recruiting Research-Centered Faculty at Non-R1 Institutions
The second session of day one will highlight best practices used by underresourced institutions to attract and retain research-capable faculty. Panelists will discuss approaches for attracting and sustaining a research-capable faculty population to advance departmental/institutional capabilities.

Moderator: **Chad Womack, Ph.D.** – United Negro College Fund (UNCF)

Panelists:
Joanna Brooks, Ph.D. – San Diego State University
Catherine K. Armwood-Gordon, Ph.D. – Tennessee State University
Ivan Mosley, Ph.D. – Tennessee State University

11:00 – 11:10 Break

11:10 – 12:10 Adapting Administrative Bandwidth for Increased Research Activity
The last session of the day will explore institutions that have successfully developed an agile and resilient administrative structure to facilitate, absorb, and efficiently manage growing funding portfolios.

Moderator: **Abraham Wolcott, Ph.D.** – San José State University

Panelists:
Almesha L. Campbell, Ph.D. – Jackson State University
Laura Collins, Ph.D. – North Carolina A&T University
Elmer Guy, Ph.D. – Navajo Technical University

12:10 – 12:15 Closing Remarks and Recapitulation of Day 1

THURSDAY, JUNE 29, 2023 (CST)

10:00 – 11:00 Barriers to Expanding the Defense Research Workforce Pipeline
The first session of day 2 will investigate challenges and opportunities for expanding workforce pipelines toward a STEM-ready research workforce. Panelists will discuss articulation programs between secondary and post-secondary institutions and necessary financial support systems and explore ways institutions across stakeholder populations can collaborate toward student matriculation into defense-research-related degrees and careers.

Moderator: **Bryn Adams, Ph.D.** – DEVCOM Army Research Laboratory

Panelists:
Shannon Arnold, M.Eng., M.S. – GBL Systems Corporation
Kerin Hilker-Balkissoon, Ph.D. – George Mason University
Charlene Mello, Ph.D. – University of Massachusetts Dartmouth

11:00 – 12:30 Challenges and Opportunities for Researchers and Personnel Engaging in Federally Funded Research
The second session of day 2 will include a panel of faculty and trainees across Minority Institution designations (HBCUs, TCU, HSIs, etc.) to discuss the challenges they face as they attempt to engage in federally funded research and spotlight opportunities for the Department of Defense, other federal agencies, and the defense industry to facilitate and sustain their participation in the respective research ecosystems.

Moderator: **Oscar Barton, Ph.D.** – Morgan State University

Panelists:
Abraham Wolcott, Ph.D. – San José State University
Saleh Zein-Sabatto, Ph.D. – Tennessee State University
Jill Keith, Ph.D. – Winston-Salem State University
Michael Groves, Ph.D. – California State University, Fullerton

12:30 – 12:40 Break

12:40 – 1:30 Federal Capacity Programs for Faculty and Trainee Support
The third session of day 2 will spotlight federal programs that provide funding to support research faculty and trainees. Representatives will highlight programs and frameworks that address independent funding opportunities, faculty teaching time, and support structures for undergrads, graduate students, and postdocs.

Moderator: **Keith McGee, Ph.D.**, Alcorn State University

Panelists:
Narcrisha S. Norman, Ph.D. – National Science Foundation
Sailaja Koduri, Ph.D. – National Institutes of Health
LaRico Treadwell, Ph.D. – Sandia National Laboratories

1:30 – 2:50 Discussion on Capacity Development and True Partnerships
The final session of day 2 will provide an overview of the topics covered throughout the workshop series, with spotlights on strategies and best practices used at academic institutions to increase research capacity building and foster equitable research partnerships.

2:50 – 3:00 Closing Remarks

Discussion leads:
Building Capacity: **Oscar Barton, Ph.D.** – Morgan State University
True Partnerships: **Chad Womack, Ph.D.** – United Negro College Fund
Federal Opportunities: **Keith McGee, Ph.D.** – Alcorn State University

- **Michael Groves, Ph.D.** –California State University, Fullerton
- **Helen Turner, Ph.D.** – Chaminade University of Honolulu

MEETING ADJOURNS

Appendix B

Town Hall Speaker Biographies

Building Defense Research Capacity at HBCUs, TCUs, HSIs, and ANNHSIs: Town Hall on Capacity Development (Transformational and Transactional Culture Shifts April 24–25, 2023)
Washington, DC (Hybrid)

MONDAY, APRIL 24, 2023 (EST)
10:10–12:00 Barriers to Building Defense-Related Research Capacity

Moderators:

Oscar Barton, Ph.D., P.E. – Morgan State University

Oscar Barton, Jr., is a professor and dean of the Morgan State University Clarence M. Mitchell, Jr. School of Engineering. A native of Washington, DC, he received his B.S. in mechanical engineering from Tuskegee (Institute) University, his M.S. in mechanical engineering, and Ph.D. in applied mechanics from Howard University in 1993. Dr. Barton joined Morgan in fall 2020, after completing 6 years at George Mason University (GMU) and a 22-year career at the U.S. Naval Academy. Dr. Barton's research focuses on the development of approximate closed form solutions for linear self-adjoint systems, those that govern the responses of composite structures, and the analysis of dynamic systems. More recently, he investigated the dynamic response of flexible composite structures subject to periodic and random excitation. He has mentored numerous midshipmen through independent research projects and has directed two Trident Scholars, the

Naval Academy's flagship research program. He has published more than 60 journal and conference articles on these topics. While at the Naval Academy and in its 163-year history, Dr. Barton was one of only three African Americans to obtain the rank of tenured full professor and the first to achieve this milestone in the Division of Engineering and Weapons, Division I. In 2010, he assumed the role of chairman of the mechanical engineering department, responsible for its strategic leadership and planning of its faculty, midshipmen-student body, curriculum, and resources. During his time as chair, the department revived and accredited the General Engineering program and created the Nuclear Engineering program, the first ever offering at the academy. Dr. Barton chaired the largest department in the Division I consisting of 42 civilian and military faculty professionals, and promoted a vibrant research and academic environment in energy and propulsion, nuclear energy, structures and materials, and design. As the founding department chair at GMU, Dr. Barton ushered growth of the department from 3 faculty and 12 students to 17 faculty and 385 undergraduate students and 6 doctoral students as of spring 2020. Under his leadership, the undergraduate program received initial EAC-ABET (Engineering Accreditation Commission–Accreditation Board for Engineering and Technology) accreditation retroactive to fall 2015, and was reaccredited to fall 2024, established state-of-the-art teaching and research labs on GMU's Sci-Tech campus, and authored an interim Ph.D. program, which is in its final stages of seeking approval from the State Council of Higher Education for Virginia. A fellow of the American Society of Mechanical Engineers (ASME), Dr. Barton is actively involved in academic innovations and program assessment. He chairs ASME's Committee on Engineering Education, is a member of ASME's Public Affairs and Outreach Council, and is a member-at-large on the Engineering Accreditation Commission's Executive Committee of ABET, after having served numerous years as a program evaluator and commissioner. He is a registered engineer licensed to practice engineering in the state of Maryland.

Abraham Wolcott, Ph.D. – San José State University

Abraham Wolcott is a physical chemist who focuses on the surface chemistry of nanoscale and bulk materials for biological labeling and alternative energy production (solar cell research). He received a B.S. and Ph.D. with Professor Jin Z. Zhang at the University of California, Santa Cruz (Jin Zhang group). He received a National Science Foundation postdoctoral fellowship and worked with Professor Xiao Yang Zhu at the University of

Texas at Austin, who then moved to Columbia University. He also worked with Profs. Jon Owen at Columbia and Dirk Englund at the Massachusetts Institute of Technology as a joint postdoctoral scientist before moving to San José State University. Prof. Wolcott has taught physical chemistry lectures (Chem 160) and laboratory (Chem 162L) and has received several grants to incorporate technology into the physical chemistry course curriculum. One pedagogical tool that is being incorporated is the use of virtual reality (VR) in the classroom. Thermodynamics, chemical kinetics, quantum mechanics, and spectroscopy are topics in which VR-based lesson plans can be developed.

Panelists

John M. Anderson, Ph.D. – Howard University

John M. Anderson holds a Ph.D. in electrical engineering from the University of Virginia, an M.S. in electrical engineering from the Georgia Institute of Technology, and an Sc.B. in electrical engineering from Brown University. After completing his doctoral studies, Dr. Anderson joined the Department of Electrical and Computer Engineering at the University of Florida. While at the University of Florida, Dr. Anderson was a visiting faculty member in the Department of Electrical and Computer Engineering at the University of Maryland in College Park. Since 2002, Dr. Anderson has been a faculty member in the Department of Electrical Engineering and Computer Science at Howard University in Washington, DC. Currently, Dr. Anderson is Dean of the Howard University College of Engineering and Architecture, as well as a professor of electrical engineering. In addition to his experiences in academia, Dr. Anderson has served as a health science administrator for the National Institute for Biomedical Imaging and Bioengineering at the National Institutes of Health and as an associate editor for the Institute of Electrical and Electronics Engineers *Signal Processing Letters*. Dr. Anderson is a National Science Foundation CAREER Award recipient and a holder of several patents.

Farin Kamangar, M.D., Ph.D. – Morgan State University

Dr. Farin Kamangar is a University Distinguished Professor and Assistant Vice President for Research at Morgan State University. He is a cancer epidemiologist, and has published over 250 peer-reviewed articles, many in top-tier journals such as *The Lancet, BMJ, Annals of Internal Medicine, Lancet Oncology, Journal of Clinical Oncology, Journal of the National Cancer Institute*, and *Gastroenterology*.

Dr. Kamangar has served as the principal investigator (PI) or co-PI of over $50 million of National Institutes of Health (NIH)-funded projects, including the ASCEND Training Model to the Enhance the Diversity of Biomedical Research Workforce, as well as major epidemiologic studies, including the Golestan Cohort Study, a large cohort study of over 50,000 individuals with over 20+ years of follow-up. He has received several research awards, including the NIH Merit Award (group award) and the National Cancer Institute Director's Innovation Award. Dr. Kamangar has collaborated with researchers at NIH, Johns Hopkins, University of Maryland, International Agency for Research on Cancer, and Tehran University of Medical Sciences, among others.

Dr. Kamangar has a passion for teaching and mentoring. He has taught at all levels, from high school to the doctoral level, and has significant experience in teaching and mentoring minority students.

Andrea Christelle, Ph.D. – Diné College

Andrea Christelle is the Vice Provost for Research at Diné College, where she fosters innovation and knowledge generation rooted in Diné values. She previously served as the acting director of Good Systems, an AI Grand Challenge at The University of Texas at Austin, and as the founding director of Philosophy in the Public Interest at Northern Arizona University.

Dr. Christelle's expertise lies in promoting and encouraging new knowledge frameworks. She is a DEI committee member for the National Council of University Research Administrators, Region VII, and serves on the editorial advisory board of the *Public Philosophy Journal*.

Dr. Christelle is the recipient of the civic leadership award for the League of Women Voters Greater Verde Valley and the American Philosophical Association/Philosophy Documentation Center's award for Excellence and Innovation in Philosophy Programs. She is a founder of Sedona Philosophy, a unique tour company that combines immersion in the natural world with philosophical reflection to advance discovery through experience and observation.

With a Ph.D. in philosophy from Tulane University and a diverse background in higher education administration, economic development, artificial intelligence ethics, and public philosophy, Dr. Christelle brings a unique and multifaceted perspective. She is committed to strengthening Diné College's research capacity by cultivating a supportive atmosphere that promotes innovation and knowledge generation rooted in Diné values. This strategy seeks to deliver cultural and economic advantages to the Navajo Nation and beyond.

Al Kuslikis – American Indian Higher Education Consortium

Al Kuslikis is Senior Associate for Strategic Initiatives at the American Indian Higher Education Consortium. An important part of Mr. Kuslikis' work involves identifying strategies for supporting science, technology, engineering, and mathematics programs at the nation's Tribal Colleges and Universities (TCUs) particularly through partnerships among the Tribal Colleges, as well as within national science and engineering research and education communities. Over the past several years, Mr. Kuslikis has been working with the national cyberinfrastructure (CI) community to develop strategies for bringing CI resources to strengthen and expand TCU STEM research and education programs. He is currently working on climate–resilience related projects supported by the Bureau of Indian Affairs, the National Science Foundation, and private foundations with a focus on environmental data science applications to support climate adaptation decision-making. Mr. Kuslikis has accumulated over 20 years of experience in American Indian higher education, beginning with his work at Diné College on the Navajo Nation. He has a background in social and cognitive science and is an ABD in Anthropology at the University of Wisconsin–Madison.

Emily Biggane, Ph.D. – United Tribes Technical College

Emily Biggane is a scientist, wife, and mother to two daughters. She grew up in Minot, North Dakota, on the traditional homelands of the Assiniboine, Anishinabewaki, Michif Piyii, and Očhéthi Šakówiŋ people. She graduated from Minot State University with a bachelor of science degree in biology in 2013 where she engaged in research on a chromosomal translocation observed in acute myeloid leukemia. Emily then attended graduate school at the University of North Dakota where her dissertation work focused on the protein, SPARC, in a model of heavy metal cadmium-induced bladder cancer. She graduated with a doctor of philosophy degree in biomedical sciences in 2019. Now, Emily is Research Faculty in the Intertribal Research and Resource Center at United Tribes Technical College (UTTC) in Bismarck, North Dakota, on the traditional homelands of the Cheyenne and Očhéthi Šakówiŋ people. They center their work around food, energy, and water sustainability for Northern Plains Tribes through research, training, education, and outreach. Emily's research broadly encompasses environmental toxicant exposures and cellular and molecular biological processes under two externally funded grants. Additionally, she prioritizes undergraduate student research, equitable partnerships, and relationship building with collaborative partners. She is a UTTC mentor for an Environmental Science Innovation and Inclusion Lab student internship through CU Boulder Earth Lab and a Purdue EPICS program project partner on an environmental dashboard project with a tribal partner. Emily also serves on the UTTC Institutional Review Board and is Vice Chair of the UTTC Data Governance committee.

Karen L. Butler-Purry, Ph.D. – Texas A&M University

Dr. Karen L. Butler-Purry was awarded a B.S. (summa cum laude) from Southern University in Baton Rouge, a M.S. degree from the University of Texas at Austin, and a Ph.D. from Howard University in Washington, D.C., all in electrical engineering. She is the first African American female to receive a Ph.D. in engineering at Howard University.

During her over 25 years at Texas A&M University, Dr. Butler-Purry has served at all faculty levels, beginning with an initial appointment as visiting assistant professor of electrical engineering in 1994. She currently is a professor in the Electrical and Computer Engineering Department. Dr. Butler-Purry has vast experiences as an administrator and program leader at Texas A&M. From 2001 to 2004, she served as Assistant Dean for Graduate Programs in the College of Engineering, served as Associate Department Head in the Electrical and Computer Engineering Department from 2008 to 2010, and served as Associate Provost for Graduate and Professional Studies from 2010 through 2020 and then in the expanded role of Associate Provost and Dean of the Graduate and Professional School through August 2022. In addition, she served as Interim Vice President for Research from 2017 to 2018.

Dr. Butler-Purry's research interests are in the areas of modeling and simulation, protection and control of electric power distribution systems and isolated power systems such as all electric power systems for ships, smart grids, and power microgrids, cybersecurity protection, intelligent systems for power system equipment deterioration and fault diagnosis, and engineering education. She is a registered professional engineer in the states of Louisiana, Texas, and Mississippi. Dr. Butler-Purry developed a successful research program and has supervised and funded nearly 50 graduate and 70 undergraduate research students. Also, she has directed several fellowship and education projects sponsored by the National Science Foundation, National Institutes of Health, and the Department of Education which promote recruitment, retention and advancement of pre-college, college, graduate students, and faculty in STEM fields, particularly individuals from historically underrepresented populations.

She received the National Science Foundation Faculty Career Award (1995) and the Office of Naval Research Young Investigator Award (1999). Dr. Butler-Purry has received numerous teaching and service awards including the 2005 American Association for the Advancement of Science Mentor Award for efforts to mentor students from underrepresented groups and for leadership in promoting Ph.D. careers for them in electrical engineering and computer sciences. She was elevated to Institute of Electrical and Electronics Engineers Fellow status in 2018. Further in 2021, Dr. Butler-Purry received the Council of Graduate Schools Debra Stewart Award for Outstanding Leadership in Graduate Education.

Frank A. Gomez, Ph.D. – Cal State System

Dr. Frank A. Gomez is the Executive Director of STEM-NET. Prior to his appointment, he was professor of chemistry at Cal State LA since 1994 and university faculty research liaison since 2014. He has received over $21 million in research funding for his work in microfluidics, point-of-care diagnostics, and fuel cells and has published over 130 technical articles and two books on his work. He has mentored over 130 undergraduate, master's, and high school students and 12 postdoctoral fellows and visiting scientists in his laboratories resulting in over 180 student presentations. He received his bachelor's in chemistry from Cal State LA and a Ph.D. in chemistry from UCLA. Dr. Gomez was a postdoctoral fellow at Harvard University. As Executive Director he has been involved in 47 proposal submissions with 21 successfully funded (involving 16 California State University [CSU] campuses) generating over $52M for the CSU system.

Folarin Erogbogbo, Ph.D. – San José State University

Folarin Erogbogbo is an American chemical engineer, scientist, and associate professor at San José State University (SJSU). He earned his Ph.D. in chemical and biological engineering from University at Buffalo (SUNY) in 2009. His dissertation was titled, "Silicon Quantum Dots and Biophotonic Applications Thereof." His teaching contributions have been to three distinct programs: chemical engineering, materials engineering, and biomedical engineering. Erogbogbo is a recognized and well-cited researcher in nanotechnology, especially in the fields of nanoparticles and cancer applications. Erogbogbo's publications have been cited 3000 times. His work is considered pioneering in nanotechnology for biomedical and energy applications because of his demonstrations with quantum dots on the nanoscale. Erogbogbo was funded by the National Science Foundation to work with Professor Mark Swihart to demonstrate the first targeted imaging of pancreatic cancer with silicon quantum dots. While funded by the Ford Foundation, Erogbogbo developed a non-toxic form of quantum dots and demonstrated their potential utility in multiple biomedical applications including, but not limited to, cancer imaging, drug delivery, and magnetic resonance imaging with Professor Paras Prasad. Erogbogbo developed the first herringbone-patterned 3D-printed reactor for nanoparticle synthesis. This reactor enables the creation of nanoparticles in a repeatable and reproducible manner. He has also worked in the social sciences areas to establish a cross-college collaboration between the biomedical engineering department and the Departments of Public Health and Sociology to provide technical social interventions that address health challenges in minority men. He has served as the chair and organizer of multiple nanotechnology symposia in the Bay Area. These include symposia titled: Nanoscience at the Molecular Foundry; Nanotechnology in Biosystems, Medicine and Health; and Nanotechnology for Energy, Healthcare and the Environment. As part of his international work, he organized a Diaspora Day Medical Panel in Nigeria. As a technical advisor, he supervises or has supervised projects at many different locations in Silicon Valley. The Silicon Valley locations include companies like Jabil Blue Sky, Covance, IRIS vision, Bioventrix, and Nutek Bravo. He has served as a technical advisor for over 50 projects. He has also supervised projects that were executed at the Stanford School of Medicine and UCSF Department of Anatomy. Erogbogbo has received multiple awards for his mentoring work with students from underrepresented minority groups. He served as the Faculty-in-Residence for the black scholars' floor at SJSU where he developed multiple initiatives to improve academic performance and social impact. He is also the advisor for the SJSU Black Alliance of Scientist and Engineers and the Nigerian Students Association Organization. He has served on committees in the Biomedical Engineering department, the Charles Davidson College of Engineering, the university, and professional organizations. Erogbogbo is a member or has been a member of the following professional organizations: Material Research Society, American Institute of Chemical Engineering, American Chemical Society, National Society of Black Engineers, American Association of Cancer Research, Biomedical Engineering Society, and the Institute of Electrical and Electronics Engineers. Erogbogbo founded Black Engineer Week (www.blackengineerweek.com) in Silicon Valley in 2021. He also Founded BEST at the TECH (www.bestatthetech.com), a partnership with San José State University and The Tech Interactive Museum.

Helen Turner, PhD – Chaminade University of Honolulu

Dr. Helen Turner serves as professor of biology and faculty in data science at Chaminade University. She is committed to Chaminade's social justice mission and works to advance equity in STEM for minoritized and marginalized individuals, especially low-income, indigenous, and veteran students. As Dean of Natural Sciences and VP for Innovation at Chaminade she led capacity-building efforts in academic excellence and inclusion over a 15-year period, including the establishment of the region's first undergraduate data science major. She was recently appointed Research Director of Chaminade's new United Nations Sustainability Center and is principal investigator of an extensive grant portfolio funded by the National Science Foundation (NSF), National Institutes of Health (NIH), the Department of Defense, and private foundations. Notably this includes leadership of a $10 million NSF INCLUDES Alliance for Hawaii-Pacific data science that spans research, education, and workforce development efforts. She also leads a prestigious Howard Hughes Medical Institute "Inclusive Excellence" program that is focused on culture, inclusion, and belonging in STEM. She serves on the leadership teams of Hawaii's statewide NIH INBRE and NSF EPSCoR programs with specific responsibilities in faculty development and DEI. Dr. Turner has led Air Force Research Laboratory– and Air Force Office of Scientific Research–funded programs in research on nanomaterial bioeffects and training (notably ROTC and veteran upskilling in data analytics) at Chaminade for over 10 years. She is a highly regarded researcher in cellular biophysics and pharmacoanalytics, loves teaching and mentoring students, and is an advocate nationally for the potential of the Pacific and its residents to be a source of models that positively inform global change.

Aaron Dotson, Ph.D. – University of Alaska Anchorage

As vice chancellor for research, Dotson's role is to support research and creative activity at University of Alaska Anchorage at all levels—from conception to completion and commercialization. To do that, the overarching Office of Research is divided into three functions, starting with the Office of Sponsored Programs, which helps researchers prepare project proposals and secure funding and awards for their work. Next is the Office of Research Integrity and Compliance, which works to maintain safety and ethicality on all projects while adhering to federal guidelines and considerations unique to Alaska. Finally, Seawolf Holdings looks to the future by supporting researchers with the licensing of intellectual property by securing patents and exploring possible commercial applications for their work. Ultimately, all three offices work in harmony to accomplish a single function.

Before formally stepping into his current role in July 2020, Dotson began working in an interim capacity starting July 2019. Even before then, Dotson was a professor and associate dean for research in the College of Engineering. Maintaining his own research portfolio, some of his projects involved wastewater treatment and providing clean water to rural Alaska communities, often collaborating with the State of Alaska, Environmental Protection Agency, and the U.S. Department of Agriculture. Fortunately, Dotson's new position will still allow him to keep his teaching and researching responsibilities, which will not only help him engage with students, but to better assess the ongoing needs of his fellow researchers.

Michele Yatchmeneff, Ph.D. – University of Alaska Anchorage

Dr. Michele Yatchemeneff is an Unangax (Aleut) woman who grew up living a traditional subsistence lifestyle in rural villages along Alaska's Aleutian chain. She was an ANSEP scholar at the University of Alaska Anchorage (UAA) where she earned a B.S. in civil engineering in 2005 and an M.S. in engineering management in 2009. After earning her B.S., she began working in Alaska's construction and engineering industry, specializing in water and sewer projects in remote villages across the state. She also worked as the Deputy Director of the Alaska Native Science and Engineering Program. Professor Yatchmeneff earned her Ph.D in engineering education from Purdue University. Her Ph.D. research focused on the motivation and success of Alaska Native pre-college STEM students. Her current research expands her doctoral work and focuses on belongingess, Alaska Native education, preparation, and retention. Professor Yatchmeneff started serving as the UAA Executive Director for Alaska Native Education and Outreach in October 2021.

12:15–1:20 Reimagining Faculty Workload Policies

Moderator:

Oscar Barton, Ph.D., P.E. – Morgan State University

Oscar Barton, Jr., is a professor and dean of the Morgan State University Clarence M. Mitchell, Jr. School of Engineering. A native of Washington, DC, he received his B.S. in mechanical engineering from Tuskegee (Institute) University, his M.S. in mechanical engineering, and Ph.D. in applied mechanics from Howard University in 1993. Dr. Barton joined Morgan in fall 2020, after completing 6 years at George Mason

University (GMU) and a 22-year career at the U.S. Naval Academy. Dr. Barton's research focuses on the development of approximate closed form solutions for linear self-adjoint systems, those that govern the responses of composite structures, and the analysis of dynamic systems. More recently, he investigated the dynamic response of flexible composite structures subject to periodic and random excitation. He has mentored numerous midshipmen through independent research projects and has directed two Trident Scholars, the Naval Academy's flagship research program. He has published more than 60 journal and conference articles on these topics. While at the Naval Academy and in its 163-year history, Dr. Barton was one of only three African Americans to obtain the rank of tenured full professor and the first to achieve this milestone in the Division of Engineering and Weapons, Division I. In 2010, he assumed the role of chairman of the mechanical engineering department, responsible for its strategic leadership and planning of its faculty, midshipmen-student body, curriculum, and resources. During his time as chair, the department revived and accredited the General Engineering program and created the Nuclear Engineering program, the first ever offering at the academy. Dr. Barton chaired the largest department in the Division I consisting of 42 civilian and military faculty professionals, and promoted a vibrant research and academic environment in energy and propulsion, nuclear energy, structures and materials, and design. As the founding department chair at GMU, Dr. Barton ushered growth of the department from 3 faculty and 12 students to 17 faculty and 385 undergraduate students and 6 doctoral students as of spring 2020. Under his leadership, the undergraduate program received initial EAC-ABET (Engineering Accreditation Commission–Accreditation Board for Engineering and Technology) accreditation retroactive to fall 2015, and was reaccredited to fall 2024, established state-of-the-art teaching and research labs on GMU's Sci-Tech campus, and authored an interim Ph.D. program, which is in its final stages of seeking approval from the State Council of Higher Education for Virginia. A fellow of the American Society of Mechanical Engineers (ASME), Dr. Barton is actively involved in academic innovations and program assessment. He chairs ASME's Committee on Engineering Education, is a member of ASME's Public Affairs and Outreach Council, and is a member-at-large on the Engineering Accreditation Commission's Executive Committee of ABET, after having served numerous years as a program evaluator and commissioner. He is a registered engineer licensed to practice engineering in the state of Maryland.

Panelists:

Mark Ginsberg, Ph.D. – George Mason University

Dr. Mark Ginsberg serves as the Provost and Executive Vice President of George Mason University, the largest public research university in Virginia and a Carnegie Research One (R1) institution. He joined George Mason University in 2010 as the dean of the College of Education and Human Development and began serving as Interim Provost and Executive Vice President on April 15, 2020. In September 2020, President Washington appointed Dr. Ginsberg as Provost and Executive Vice President of George Mason University.

From January 1999 until June 2010, Dr. Ginsberg served as the Executive Director and Chief Executive Officer of the National Association for the Education of Young Children (NAEYC). Prior to joining NAEYC, Dr. Ginsberg was chair of the Department of Counseling and Human Services in the Graduate Division of Education at The Johns Hopkins University and a member of the faculty of both the Department of Psychiatry and Behavioral Sciences and the Department of Medicine in the School of Medicine. He had served as a member of the Hopkins full-time and part-time faculty for more than 25 years. Before joining Johns Hopkins, Dr. Ginsberg held the position of Executive Director of the American Association for Marriage and Family Therapy (AAMFT) from 1986 to 1993. From 1981 to 1986, he was a senior member of the management staff of the American Psychological Association (APA) after having been a faculty member in the Department of Psychology at the University of Rochester.

Dr. Ginsberg serves as the Chair of the Board of Directors of the respected international organization, Parents as Teachers. He also serves on the Board of Directors of the Association of Chief Academic Officers, the national organization of university provosts, as well as Hopecam, a non-profit organization that supports children with cancer and their families and as an appointed member of the Fairfax County (Virginia) Successful Children and Youth Policy Team. He is a Past-Chair of the Board of Directors of the American Association of Colleges for Teacher Education and had served as a member of the Executive Committee of the Council of Academic Deans of Research Education Institutions and the Board of Directors of the Virginia Early Childhood Foundation. He also is a past-president of both the International Step by Step Association, a group of education and child/youth development–focused nongovernmental organizations in Europe and Central Asia, and the Society of Psychologists in Management.

He is a Fellow of both the APA and the Maryland Psychological Association, and a Clinical Member and Fellow of the AAMFT.

Dr. Ginsberg completed his master's degree in 1978 and his doctoral degree in 1981 at The Pennsylvania State University, after having been awarded a bachelor's degree from the State University of New York at Cortland in 1975. He also completed a Fellowship in Clinical Psychology at the Yale University School of Medicine. In 2006, he was awarded the honorary degree of doctor of humane letters by the State University of New York.

John Crockett, Ph.D. – San Diego State University

John Crockett contributes to the health of San Diego State University's (SDSU's) Research Enterprise by attending to the needs of the complete research community, including the goals and aspirations of faculty, non-faculty researchers, postdocs, graduate students, and undergraduate students.

John Crockett is the Associate Vice President for Research Advancement in the Division of Research and Innovation at San Diego State University. Dr. Crockett's team is responsible for curating and amplifying the research reputation of SDSU at the institutional level. Dr. Crockett maintains two research programs, one focused on ethnic, racial, and gender diversity in STEM higher education, and the second on the formation and function of teams, related to team science enterprises. Dr. Crockett is an expert on early-career faculty success, and an invited speaker for major university systems across the country and state and federal agencies including the California Energy Commission, NASA, U.S. Department of Agriculture, and the Department of Defense, to name a few examples. Dr. Crockett received a bachelor of arts in earth and environmental science from Wesleyan University, and an M.S. and Ph.D. in marine geology from the University of Washington.

1:30–2:45 Culture and Leadership Models to Facilitate Research Capacity Building

Moderator:

Abigail S. Newsome, Ph.D. – Mississippi Valley State University

Abigail S. Newsome, a native of Itta Bena, Mississippi, attended Leflore County High School. After her graduation, she studied biology at Mississippi Valley State University (MVSU) and later attended the University of Southern Mississippi where she obtained her Ph.D. in biology with a concentration in molecular biology. She then began her professional tenure at Mississippi Valley State University in August of 1997, where she began teaching biology and microbiology in the Department of Natural Sciences and Environmental Health. During this time, she worked closely with the MVSU Football Team serving as film/video coordinator. Dr. Newsome has also served as a visiting professor of biology at the University of the Virgin Islands in St. Thomas, U.S. Virgin Islands, and has engaged in various collaborations and partnerships at universities across the country and abroad. Dr. Newsome presently serves as Mississippi Valley State University's faculty athletics representative. Her academic position at MVSU is the director of bioinformatics where her efforts are focused on graduate education and research in genomics. Dr. Newsome and her husband, Dr. Albert L. Love, have three adult children and two grandsons.

Abraham Wolcott, Ph.D. – San José State University

Abraham Wolcott is a physical chemist who focuses on the surface chemistry of nanoscale and bulk materials for biological labeling and alternative energy production (solar cell research). He received a B.S. and Ph.D. with Professor Jin Z. Zhang at the University of California, Santa Cruz (Jin Zhang group). He received a National Science Foundation postdoctoral fellowship and worked with Professor Xiao Yang Zhu at the University of Texas at Austin, who then moved to Columbia University. He also worked with Profs. Jon Owen at Columbia and Dirk Englund at the Massachusetts Institute of Technology as a joint postdoctoral scientist before moving to San José State University. Prof. Wolcott has taught physical chemistry lectures (Chem 160) and laboratory (Chem 162L) and has received several grants to incorporate technology into the physical chemistry course curriculum. One pedagogical tool that is being incorporated is the use of virtual reality (VR) in the classroom. Thermodynamics, chemical kinetics, quantum mechanics, and spectroscopy are topics in which VR-based lesson plans can be developed.

Panelists:

Jagannathan Sankar, Ph.D. – North Carolina A&T University

Professor Sankar over the past 36 years has developed a high-profile, internationally recognized, advanced broad-based materials innovation and technology activities at North Carolina A&T State University (NCAT), Greensboro, North Carolina. He serves or has served as director of the Center for Advanced Materials and Smart Structures, National Science Foundation (NSF) CREST program, Director for the Navy Center for Nanoscience and Nanomaterials, and site coordinator for the NSF Nanoscale Science and Engineering Center. Also under his leadership, NCAT was chosen (2008) to house the NSF's Generation 3 Engineering Research Center (ERC) for Revolutionizing Metallic Biomaterials. The ERCs are considered the crown jewel of NSF and only select few universities over the past 40 years have been awarded after a gargantuan competition to conduct transformational and revolutionary engineering innovation for the economic impact and global leadership of the nation. Through these centers, Sankar and the international team of collaborators he has assembled over the years have positioned NCAT in various leading advanced materials research and developments through innovative public-private partnerships, surface engineering, convergence of engineering and science in transformational biomedical implant technologies. The author of more than 400 peer-reviewed articles, book chapters, and scientific papers, Sankar as principal investigator alone has generated more than $60 million of competitive research funding for NCAT (equipment infrastructure > $14 million under one umbrella encompassing 25,000 square feet of innovation ecosystem space), filed ten invention disclosures and patents, has organized and sponsored more than 25 international conferences/symposia, and has given more than 35 plenary/keynote/invited special addresses in major get-togethers this decade related to future directions in transformational materials and nano/bio research, education, innovation, economic impact and growth, and next generation workforce development. He also played a key role in establishing the B.S. and M.S. bioengineering degree programs at NCAT, the first stand-alone at an HBCU in the nation. Dr. Sankar is leading a sincere effort in adding value to American knowledge economy through innovation, translation, manufacturing technologies in broad-based materials with underpinning innovative education, outreach, and broadened participation.

Twyla Baker, Ph.D. – Neurta Hidatsa Sahnish College

Dr. Twyla Baker is an enrolled citizen of the Mandan, Hidatsa & Arikara Nation of North Dakota. Born and raised on the Fort Berthold Indian Reservation, Dr. Baker left home for several years and built a life away from the reservation, though she maintained strong ties to her home community. She returned home in 2013 to work for her Tribe's institution of higher education, and currently serves as the President of Nueta Hidatsa Sahnish College. Viewing life through an Indigenous lens, her world view informs nearly everything she does professionally and personally, and she is raising her children to live in their identities as contemporary Native people and carry on their Tribal lifeways as they were taught to her by her own parents, family, and community. She has spent a lifetime establishing her credibility among her Tribal people and with external constituencies through research, advocacy, education, community engagement, and activism. Dr. Baker has published creative and scholarly works in various media, and has made appearances on CNN, MSNBC, NBC, NPR, and internationally on BBC and Australian television giving commentary and insight on numerous topics impacting Indian Country in the United States.

TUESDAY, APRIL 25, 2023 (EST)
10:00–11:30 Developing a Diverse Funding Portfolio

Moderator:

Oscar Barton, Ph.D., P.E. – Morgan State University

Oscar Barton, Jr., is a professor and dean of the Morgan State University Clarence M. Mitchell, Jr. School of Engineering. A native of Washington, DC, he received his B.S. in mechanical engineering from Tuskegee (Institute) University, his M.S. in mechanical engineering, and Ph.D. in applied mechanics from Howard University in 1993. Dr. Barton joined Morgan in fall 2020, after completing 6 years at George Mason University (GMU) and a 22-year career at the U.S. Naval Academy. Dr. Barton's research focuses on the development of approximate closed form solutions for linear self-adjoint systems, those that govern the responses of composite structures, and the analysis of dynamic systems. More recently, he investigated the dynamic response of flexible composite structures subject to periodic and random excitation. He has mentored numerous midshipmen through independent research projects and has directed two Trident Scholars, the Naval Academy's flagship research program. He has published more than 60 journal and conference articles on these topics. While at the Naval Academy and in its 163-year history, Dr. Barton was one of only three African Americans to obtain the rank of tenured full professor and the first to achieve this milestone in the Division of Engineering and Weapons, Division I. In 2010, he assumed the role of chairman of the mechanical engineering department, responsible for its strategic leadership and planning of its faculty, midshipmen-student body, curriculum, and resources. During his time as chair, the department revived and accredited the General Engineering program and created the Nuclear Engineering program, the first ever offering at the academy. Dr. Barton chaired the largest department in the Division I consisting of 42 civilian and military faculty professionals, and promoted a vibrant research and academic environment in energy and propulsion, nuclear energy, structures and materials, and design. As the founding department chair at GMU, Dr. Barton ushered growth of the department from 3 faculty and 12 students to 17 faculty and 385 undergraduate students and 6 doctoral students as of spring 2020. Under his leadership, the undergraduate program received initial EAC-ABET (Engineering Accreditation Commission–Accreditation Board for Engineering and Technology) accreditation retroactive to fall 2015, and was reaccredited to fall 2024, established state-of-the-art teaching and research labs on GMU's Sci-Tech campus, and authored an interim Ph.D. program, which is in its final stages of seeking approval from the State Council of Higher Education for Virginia. A fellow of the American Society of Mechanical Engineers (ASME), Dr. Barton is actively involved in academic innovations and program assessment. He chairs ASME's Committee on Engineering Education, is a member of ASME's Public Affairs and Outreach Council, and is a member-at-large on the Engineering Accreditation Commission's Executive Committee of ABET, after having served numerous years as a program evaluator and commissioner. He is a registered engineer licensed to practice engineering in the state of Maryland.

Panelist:
Kamal H. Khayat, Ph.D. – Missouri University of Science and Technology

Kamal H. Khayat is the Vice-Chancellor for Research and Innovation and the Vernon and Maralee Jones Professor of Civil Engineering at Missouri S&T. Between August 2011 and June 2014, he directed the Center for Transportation Infrastructure and Safety, a National University Transportation Center (UTC). The $37 million grant funded 174 research, equipment, and education projects. He also directed the Tier-1 UTC, Research on Concrete Applications for Sustainable Transportation between September 2013 and December 2019 and the Missouri S&T Center for Infrastructure Engineering Studies between August 2011 and October 2021. He led efforts to establish the Clayco Advanced Construction and Materials Laboratory, a 1,375-m^2 state-of-the-art research facility inaugurated in 2020.

Dr. Khayat has conducted pioneer work in the field of rheology of cement-based materials and self-consolidating concrete. Other research interests include ultra-high-performance concrete, fiber-reinforced composites, infrastructure rehabilitation, and grouting.

Professor Khayat has chaired/co-chaired several international conferences, including the 2020 Gordon Research Conference (Ventura Beach, California), SCC2016 (Washington, DC), and SCC2010 (Montreal). His creative contributions to innovation, leadership, and technology transfer have been recognized by several international organizations including the 2020 University of Missouri System President's Award for Sustained Career Excellence in STEM/Natural Sciences, the 2020 Robert E. Philleo Award, the 2018 Wason Medal, the 2017 J.-C. Roumain Award, and the 2015 Arthur Anderson Medal from the American Concrete Institute.

Professor Khayat was awarded over 135 research projects with approximate funding of approximately $31 million as principal investigator (PI) and $13 million as co-PI. He has advised 40 Ph.D. students, 44 M.Sc. students, and 22 postdoctoral fellows and visiting scholars and has co-authored over 500 publications, 11 contributions to books and book chapters, and served as editor/co-editor of 19 books and conference proceedings. Dr. Khayat earned a B.S. in civil engineering in 1982, M.Eng. in construction engineering and management in 1984, M.S. in structural engineering in 1985, and Ph.D. in civil engineering in 1989 from the University of California, Berkeley.

11:30–12:30 Addressing the Critical Threshold for Infrastructure Investments

Moderator:

Chad Womack, Ph.D. – United Negro College Fund

Chad Womack is the senior director of National STEM Programs and Initiatives. Prior to joining the United Negro College Fund (UNCF), Dr. Womack co-founded the America21 Project and DC Innovates, both innovation-based community and economic development nonprofit organizations dedicated to empowering metro-centers and underserved communities through STEM education, tech-entrepreneurship, and access to capital. In addition, Dr. Womack led the White House–based Historically Black Colleges and Universities (HBCU) Startup and Innovation Initiative, which resulted in the launch of the HBCU Innovation, Commercialization and Entrepreneurship initiative at UNCF. At UNCF, Dr. Womack's work portfolio includes the Fund II Foundation STEM Scholars Program—a $50 million and 10-year commitment to support 500 academically talented African American high school students pursuing STEM as majors in college and careers in the technology industry; the Ernest E. Just Life Sciences

Institute, which includes the Bristol-Myers Squibb–sponsored EE Just Life Sciences Postgraduate Fellowship Program; the UNCF HBCU Innovation, Commercialization and Entrepreneurship Initiative; the UNCF HBCU Innovation Summit and the HBCU Center of Excellence in Computing and Computer Science, which includes a partnership with Google. Dr. Womack was previously a member of the U.S. Department of Commerce, Economic Development Agency, National Advisory Council for Innovation and Entrepreneurship, and the D.C. Mayor's Innovation and Technology Inclusion Council. Dr. Womack completed several postdoctoral research fellowships at the National Institutes of Health in the National Institutes for Allergy and Infectious Diseases Vaccine Research Center, and at the Harvard AIDS Institute and the Harvard School of Public Health in the Department of Immunology and Infectious Diseases. Dr. Womack earned his doctoral degree in biomedical sciences from the Morehouse School of Medicine and is a proud graduate of Morehouse College, where he majored in biology with minors in chemistry and applied physics.

Panelists

Shannon Arnold, M.Eng., M.S. – GBL Systems Corporation

Shannon Arnold is a Principle Scientist at GBL Systems Corporation. Mr. Arnold is a prolific engineer with over 30 years of experience working in government and industry serving as research and development engineering in organizations such as the National Aeronautics and Space Administration and the Scientific Research Corporation. His work and passion has also included identifying opportunities to broaden defense-related research and development opportunities for individuals from underrepresented communities. Mr. Arnold earned a B.S. in chemistry and mathematics from Morehouse College in 1992, a M.S. in organic and polymer chemistry from Clark Atlanta University in 1994, and a M.Eng. from Virginia Tech in 1998.

Victor R. McCrary, Ph.D. – University of the District of Columbia

Victor R. McCrary, Vice President for Research at the University of the District of Columbia (UDC), is an advocate for the growth, development, and strategic direction of the University's research enterprise. UDC is the nation's capital only public institution of higher education to offer students degree opportunities from 2-year, 4-year, graduate and law school degrees and research opportunities that offer hands experience in urban sustainability and resiliency. UDC is "DC's Research Laboratory." He is also the current Vice Chair of the National Science Board, the governing body for the National Science Foundation. In October 2016, President Barack Obama appointed Dr. McCrary to serve on the National Science Board. In May 2022, Dr. McCrary was re-appointed by President Joseph Biden to a 6-year term on the National Science Board. He is a change agent and serial innovator, always seeking to make a difference by unlocking the creative potential in individuals and organizations. He has held executive positions at the Johns Hopkins University Applied Physics Laboratory, Morgan State University, and as division chief at the National Institute of Standards and Technology (NIST). His accomplishments include the development of the first industry-led electronic book standards and an electronic book Braille reader which led to him being co-recipient of the U.S. Department of Commerce's Gold Medal in 2000. Dr. McCrary served 6 years as the national president of the National Organization for the Professional Advancement of Black Chemists and Chemical Engineers and was awarded the organization's 2002 Percy Julian Award. He is a Fellow of the American Chemical Society. In 2011, he was honored as Scientist of the Year by the Annual Black Engineer of the Year Award STEM Conference. He received his doctoral degree in chemistry from Howard University in 1985, a master's degree in engineering from the University of Pennsylvania in 1995, and a bachelor's degree in chemistry from The Catholic University of America in 1978.

Dr. McCrary enjoys mentoring students and the next generation of research and technology professionals in order that they look to give back to their communities and seek to make a positive change in the world for all. He is a member of the Knights of Columbus, and his council over the past decade has raised over $200,000 for the Tanzanian Children's Fund to dig wells for water and to build medical facilities.

Jaret C. Riddick, Ph.D. – Center for Security and Emerging Technology

Dr. Jaret C. Riddick is a Senior Fellow at Georgetown University's Center for Security and Emerging Technology (CSET). Prior to joining CSET, he was the Principal Director for Autonomy in the Office of the Under Secretary for Research and Engineering (OUSD(R&E)), serving as the senior Department of Defense (DOD) official for coordination, strategy, and transition of Autonomy research and development. As Principal Director, he created a DOD-wide initiative on trusted Autonomy, led efforts to advance Autonomy for undersea warfare with allied partners, and provided key strategic analysis to support development of the newest DOD University Affiliated Research Center. Prior to OUSD(R&E), Jaret served in executive leadership roles in the U.S. Army Research Laboratory (ARL), where he established a 200-acre robotics research collaboration campus and led ARL senior leadership efforts to establish the research competencies of the Laboratory. He has also served in leadership roles in the Office of the Deputy Assistant Secretary of the Army for Research and Technology, and the former Office of the Under Secretary of Defense for Acquisition, Technology and Logistics. He holds a Ph.D. in engineering mechanics from Virginia Tech, M.S. in mechanical engineering from North Carolina A&T State University, and B.S. in mechanical engineering from Howard University.

1:30–2:30 Federal Capacity-Building Programs

Moderator:

Keith A. McGee, Ph.D. – Alcorn State University

Keith A. McGee, a native of Quitman, located in Clarke County, Mississippi, began his postsecondary education at Mississippi Valley State University, majoring in biology and culminating with a Ph.D. from the University of Southern Mississippi in molecular biology. Dr. McGee's research focused on a family of ATP (adenosine triphosphate) transport proteins, specifically those involved in phenotypic multidrug resistance. As a faculty member, he sustained a productive graduate student training program, advising many master's degree–seeking students, along with many undergraduates, and summer research students. Dr. McGee has served in multiple administrative capacities at Alcorn State University; most recently he was appointed to serve as the inaugural associate provost for research, innovation, and graduate education. In this role, Dr. McGee is responsible for providing leadership in developing a clear research vision and growing the university's research footprint while leading and elevating the university's interdisciplinary research activities. Dr. McGee is charged with promoting an understanding and drive for new research opportunities, working with the university deans on all aspects of research and graduate education to ensure alignment with their specific disciplines, while supporting and expanding innovative graduate programs and scholarly activity.

Panelists:

Natalia Melcer – Department of Energy, Office of Science

Natalia Melcer is a Senior Technical Advisor in the Office of the Deputy Director for Science Programs, Office of Science, Department of Energy (DOE). In this position, she provides strategic advice on all aspects of science program management, including program planning, budget formulation, execution, and evaluation. She provides advice and assistance in the formulation and implementation of new policies, plans, and procedures regarding the Office of Science program offices and DOE national laboratories. She previously served as a program manager in the DOE Office of Science, Office of Basic Energy Sciences, with primary duties related to budget formulation, strategic planning, and communications. Earlier in her career, she served as Assistant Deputy Director in the DOE Office of Budget, Office of the Chief Financial Officer, where she developed DOE budgetary policy. She previously served as a Senior Program Officer with the Board on Physics and Astronomy at the National Academies and as a Science Policy Fellow working in the Office of Legislative and Government Affairs at the American Chemical Society. She holds a B.S. in applied chemistry from the University of Calgary and a M.S. in chemistry from the University of Michigan.

Dina Myers Stroud, Ph.D. – National Science Foundation, GRANTED program

Dina Myers Stroud joined the National Science Foundation from Vanderbilt and Fisk Universities. Passionate about building research access and capacity, especially at Minority Serving Institutions, Dina works in the Office of Integrative Activities as Lead Program Director for GRANTED and HBCU-Excellence in Research. Dina acquired her Ph.D. in molecular biology from Vanderbilt with a focus on developmental biology. Dr. Stroud did postdoctoral work in cardiovascular research at the University of California, Los Angeles, New York University, and the Vanderbilt University Medical Center, initially working in heart development and moving into the genetics of arrythmias. As the Executive Director of the Fisk-Vanderbilt Master's to PhD Bridge Program (FVBP), Dr. Stroud advocated for and mentored students from underrepresented and underserved groups into and through STEM Ph.D. programs and the workforce. She oversaw formalization and dissemination of practices, as well as building mutually beneficial partnerships, and building diverse, inclusive community. This experience led her to work with the National Institutes of Heath–sponsored National Research Mentoring Network as part of the original team creating mentor-mentee supportive technology known as MyNRMN. Dr. Stroud also served as the Director of the National Science Foundation Louis Stokes Alliances for Minority Participation (LSAMP) Regional Center of Excellence in Broadening Participation. She directed educational research centered on the FVBP, in collaboration with the Peabody School of Education at Vanderbilt and the American Institutes for Research.

Building Defense Research Capacity at HBCUs, TCUs, HSIs, and ANNHSIs: Town Hall on True Partnerships (May 22–23, 2023)
Albuquerque, New Mexico (Hybrid)

MONDAY, MAY 22, 2023 (MST)
10:30–11:30 Igniting the Defense Research Ecosystem

Moderator:

Melvin Greer, Ph.D. – Intel Corporation

Melvin Greer is chief data scientist, Americas, Intel Corporation. Dr. Greer is responsible for building Intel's data science platform through artificial intelligence, machine learning, and neuromorphic computing to accelerate transformation of data into a strategic asset for global enterprises. His systems and software engineering experience has resulted in patented inventions in cloud computing, synthetic biology, and IoT (Internet of Things) biosensors for edge analytics. He functions as a university professor and principal investigator where he significantly advances the body of knowledge in basic research and advanced engineering. Dr. Greer is one of the 2018 LinkedIn Top 10 Voices in data science and analytics. He also received the WashingtonExec inaugural Pinnacle Award as the 2018 Artificial Intelligence Executive of the Year. He received the 2017 BDPA (Black Data Processing Associates) Lifetime Achievement Award and the 2012 BEYA (Black Engineer of the Year Award) Technologist of the Year Award, which recognize his outstanding technical contributions that have had a material impact and high value to society as a whole. Dr. Greer is a member of the American Association for the Advancement of Science and has served for 8 years on the National Academies' Government University Industry Research Roundtable. He has been appointed senior advisor and fellow at the Federal Bureau of Investigation (FBI) Information Technology and Data Division. He is charged with the acceleration of the FBI mission by supporting appropriate data collection, data analytics, discovery, and visualization via advanced data science and artificial intelligence techniques.

Panelists:

Victor McCrary, Ph.D. – University of the District of Columbia

Victor R. McCrary, Vice President for Research at the University of the District of Columbia (UDC), is an advocate for the growth, development, and strategic direction of the University's research enterprise. UDC is the nation's capital only public institution of higher education to offer students degree opportunities from 2-year, 4-year, graduate and law school degrees and research opportunities that offer hands experience in urban sustainability and resiliency. UDC is “DC’s Research Laboratory.” He is also the current Vice Chair of the National Science Board, the governing body for the National Science Foundation. In October 2016, President Barack Obama appointed Dr. McCrary to serve on the National Science Board. In May 2022, Dr. McCrary was re-appointed by President Joseph Biden to a 6-year term on the National Science Board. He is a change agent and serial innovator, always seeking to make a difference by unlocking the creative potential in individuals and organizations. He has held executive positions at the Johns Hopkins University Applied Physics Laboratory, Morgan State University, and as division chief at the National Institute of Standards and Technology (NIST). His accomplishments include the development of the first industry-led electronic book standards and an electronic book Braille reader which led to him being co-recipient of the U.S. Department of Commerce’s Gold Medal in 2000. Dr. McCrary served 6 years as the national president of the National Organization for the Professional Advancement of Black Chemists and Chemical Engineers and was awarded the organization’s 2002 Percy Julian Award. He is a Fellow of the American Chemical Society. In 2011, he was honored as Scientist of the Year by the Annual Black Engineer of the Year Award STEM Conference. He received his doctoral degree in chemistry from Howard University in 1985, a master’s degree in engineering from the University of Pennsylvania in 1995, and a bachelor’s degree in chemistry from The Catholic University of America in 1978.

Dr. McCrary enjoys mentoring students and the next generation of research and technology professionals in order that they look to give back to their communities and seek to make a positive change in the world for all. He is a member of the Knights of Columbus, and his council over the past decade has raised over $200,000 for the Tanzanian Children’s Fund to dig wells for water and to build medical facilities.

Santosh Devasia, Ph.D. – University of Washington

Santosh Devasia received a B.Tech. (Hons.) from the Indian Institute of Technology, Kharagpur, India, in 1988, and M.S. and Ph.D. degrees in mechanical engineering from the University of California at Santa Barbara in 1990 and 1993, respectively. He joined the University of Washington Department of Mechanical Engineering in 2000. In addition to directing the Precision Controls Laboratory, he serves as the associate director of the Boeing Advanced Research Center at the University of Washington, which focuses on the manufacturing and assembly of aircraft and spacecraft structures.

Thomas Tubon – BioMADE

Thomas Tubon is the chief workforce development officer for BioMADE. Prior to his appointment with BioMADE, he served as a professor in the Biotechnology Program at Madison Area Technical College for 13 years. During this time, he led several National Science Foundation (NSF) Advanced Technological Education initiatives to establish and scale an emerging technology program in stem cells and cell manufacturing and directed a National Coordination Network in Advanced Manufacturing of Cell and Tissue Products. While at Madison College, Dr. Tubon was responsible for the development of bioscience workforce and strategic implementation of programs for local-, regional-, and national-level adoption and scale-up. In this role, he has facilitated the creation of a broad network of industry, community, and academic stakeholders designed to foster career pathways in STEM. He also serves as a mentor with the NSF Advanced Technological Education (ATE) Mentor Connect and Project Vision Programs. Dr. Tubon held leadership roles with the NSF ATE InnovATEBIO Center for Biotechnology Education, and the NSF Advancing Research Impact in Society Center with a focus on education, workforce development, and strategic partnerships. Dr. Tubon holds a Ph.D. in molecular genetics from Stony Brook University and Cold Spring Harbor Laboratory and a B.S. in molecular biology from San Diego State University.

11:50–12:50 Articulating the Value Proposition for Equitable Partnerships

Moderator:

Oscar Barton, Ph.D., P.E. – Morgan State University

Oscar Barton, Jr., is a professor and dean of the Morgan State University Clarence M. Mitchell, Jr. School of Engineering. A native of Washington, DC, he received his B.S. in mechanical engineering from Tuskegee (Institute) University, his M.S. in mechanical engineering, and Ph.D. in applied mechanics from Howard University in 1993. Dr. Barton joined Morgan in fall 2020, after completing 6 years at George Mason University (GMU) and a 22-year career at the U.S. Naval Academy. Dr. Barton's research focuses on the development of approximate closed form solutions for linear self-adjoint systems, those that govern the responses of composite structures, and the analysis of dynamic systems. More recently, he investigated the dynamic response of flexible composite structures subject to periodic and random excitation. He has mentored numerous midshipmen through independent research projects and has directed two Trident Scholars, the Naval Academy's flagship research program. He has published more than 60 journal and conference articles on these topics. While at the Naval Academy and in its 163-year history, Dr. Barton was one of only three African Americans to obtain the rank of tenured full professor and the first to achieve this milestone in the Division of Engineering and Weapons, Division I. In 2010, he assumed the role of chairman of the mechanical engineering department, responsible for its strategic leadership and planning of its faculty, midshipmen-student body, curriculum, and resources. During his time as chair, the department revived and accredited the General Engineering program and created the Nuclear Engineering program, the first ever offering at the academy. Dr. Barton chaired the largest department in the Division I consisting of 42 civilian and military faculty professionals, and promoted a vibrant research and academic environment in energy and propulsion, nuclear energy, structures and materials, and design. As the founding department chair at GMU, Dr. Barton ushered growth of the department from 3 faculty and 12 students to 17 faculty and 385 undergraduate students and 6 doctoral students as of spring 2020. Under his leadership, the undergraduate program received initial EAC-ABET (Engineering Accreditation Commission–Accreditation Board for Engineering and Technology) accreditation retroactive to fall 2015, and was reaccredited to fall 2024, established state-of-the-art teaching and research labs on GMU's Sci-Tech campus, and authored an interim Ph.D. program, which is in its final stages of seeking approval from the State Council of Higher Education for Virginia. A fellow of the American Society of Mechanical Engineers (ASME), Dr. Barton is actively involved in academic innovations and program assessment. He chairs ASME's Committee on Engineering Education, is a member of ASME's Public Affairs and Outreach Council, and is a member-at-large on the Engineering Accreditation Commission's Executive Committee of ABET, after having served numerous years as a program evaluator and commissioner. He is a registered engineer licensed to practice engineering in the state of Maryland.

Panelists:

Eric Adolphe, Esq. – Forward Edge-AI, Inc.

Eric Adolphe is CEO of Forward Edge-AI, Inc. Of Haitian heritage, he is a technology-savvy executive with more than 30 years of success building high-growth firms focused on mission impact, revenue, and margin attainment. Mr. Adolphe leverages expertise in deep technology including artificial intelligence/machine learning, quantum encryption, and blockchain/distributed ledger technology to solve complex social, public safety, and national security challenges. As principal investigator under a NASA Small Business Innovative Research (SBIR) program, he developed a data analytics solution designed to facilitate the interpretation of large volumes of data that can be retrieved from distributed sources to provide a highly efficient method to extract causal factors underlying aerospace mishaps attributable to human factors. Each source providing data on aerospace mishaps was modeled as an information retrieval system. A uniform identification scheme—based on a uniform resource identifier, or UFI, made up of descriptors from a controlled set—would be used to encode the "raw data," thus ensuring comparability in data reports from different sources. He has led cross-disciplinary research/research and development teams (biology, computation, chemistry, engineering, psychology) of typically 3 to 28 researchers on 25 SBIRs over his career. His products have been installed in every air traffic control facility in the United States. Mr. Adolphe's Earth Polychromatic Imaging Camera (EPIC) SBIR won NASA's Most Innovative SBIR Software Product of the Year award. As a result, he received one of NASA's highest civilian commendations, and is one of 11 Black American honorees at the National Inventors Hall of Fame. EPIC is in use today by the commercial space launch industry. Mr. Adolphe also developed a DNN (deep neural network) to detect aircraft in high clutter radar images (ASDE-X [Airport Surface Detection Equipment, Model X] radar), under Phase I/II SBIR projects for the U.S. Department of Transportation/Volpe Center. He holds a bachelor of engineering degree in electrical engineering from City University of New York's City College of New York and is a cum laude graduate from Catholic University of America, Columbus School of Law, and a member of the Maryland Bar. Mr. Adolphe is a winner of the Maryland High Tech Entrepreneur of the Year award. He is also a National Capital Business Ethics and Service to the Citizens awards winner, and National Inventors Hall of Fame honoree. He is also a winner of one of NASA's highest civilian honors, and is an SBIR Tibbetts award winner.

Christina Deckard – Office of the Under Secretary of Defense, Biotechnology

Christina "Chris" Deckard is senior scientist at SAIC (Science Applications International Corporation) with the Office of the Under Secretary of Defense for Research and Engineering, Biotechnology. She has also served as director of military and veteran services at Dallas Baptist University. Her department works with more than 300 military-affiliated students per semester. She also serves as a member of the Veterans Business Alliance for the Arlington, Texas, Chamber of Commerce. Ms. Deckard is a veteran of the U.S. Air Force and holds a master's degree in organizational leadership from Waldorf University.

Robert St. Amant, Ph.D. – DEVCOM Army Research Laboratory

Robert St. Amant is a computer scientist with the U.S. Army DEVCOM Army Research Laboratory. His B.S. is in electric engineering and computer science from Johns Hopkins University, and his Ph.D. is in computer science from the University of Massachusetts. He was a professor in the Department of Computer Science at North Carolina State University. He received the 2013 Outstanding Teacher of the Year Award from the NC State College of Engineering. He has written papers on human-computer interaction, cognitive science, artificial intelligence, and the use of tools by nonhuman animals; his popular science book, *Computing for Ordinary Mortals*, was published by Oxford in 2012.

1:10–2:10 Models for Synergistic Partnerships

Moderator:

Bryn L. Adams, Ph.D. – DEVCOM Army Research Laboratory

Bryn L. Adams received a B.S. in biology in 2001 and a Ph.D. in interdisciplinary biology in 2009 from the University of North Carolina at Charlotte. Her doctoral studies included a variety of research projects in the field of applied and environmental microbiology. Dr. Adams completed two postdoctoral fellowships; the first was a collaborative project, as a National Academy of Sciences postdoctoral fellow, between DEVCOM Chemical Biological Center and the Institute of Bioscience and Biotechnology Research at the University of Maryland, College Park, which focused on the development of nonspecific threat agent detection using simple biological sensing and signal transduction pathways. The second fellowship was with DEVCOM Army Research Laboratory as an Oak Ridge Associated

Universities postdoctoral fellow, where she conducted research into the development of synthetic molecular recognition agents for biosensing and biomaterials. In 2014, Dr. Adams converted to a federal civilian research scientist at the Army Research Lab. She has led the Synbio Tools and Chassis Team in the Biotechnology Branch since 2018. Her research efforts currently focus on developing synthetic biology tools for nonmodel host bacteria and establishing the capability of synthetic biology from the lab and into the hands of the warfighter. She has published more than 20 peer-reviewed manuscripts on a wide range of bacterial biotechnology topics across several disciplines and was awarded the Department of Defense (DOD) Scientist of the Quarter in 2019 for her contributions to the field of biotechnology for DOD. Dr. Adams is currently on a 1-year detail assignment to the Office of the Under Secretary of Defense for Research and Engineering, where she leads the Education and Workforce Development component of the Biotechnology Modernization Priority.

Panelists:

Kelly Freidenfelds, Ph.D. – Princeton-HBCU Alliance for Collaborative Research

As senior associate director of foundation relations, Dr. Freidenfelds works to build stronger relationships with foundations and other partners in support of faculty research and university priorities. She specializes in supporting the humanities, social sciences, natural sciences and diversity, equity and inclusion, as well as organizations central to campus life such as the Princeton University Library, Princeton University Art Museum, and the Office of Religious Life. Before joining the Office of Corporate Engagement and Foundation Relations, Dr. Freidenfelds served as manager of corporate, foundation, and government relations at the Princeton University Art Museum. Prior to coming to Princeton, she supported development efforts at the Kingsborough Community College Foundation of the City University of New York, New York University Stern School of Business, and the Bard Graduate Center. She has presented with NCURA (National Council of University Research Administrators), SRAI (Society of Research Administrators International), and CASE (Council for the Advancement and Support of Education) and has served on the organizing committee for the CASE Corporate and Foundation Relations conference. Dr. Freidenfelds holds a Ph.D. in cultural anthropology from Stanford University and a B.A. from Wesleyan University. She lives in Princeton and recently served on the board of the Princeton Public Library Foundation.

Robert Louis Shepard, Ph.D. – The Shepard Institute, LLC

Robert Louis Shepard has pushed hard for increased participation of faculty and students from Historically Black Colleges and Universities (HBCUs) in the federal government's research enterprise. He is principal at The Shepard Institute (TSI), LLC. TSI mentoring services are offered to underutilized academic institutions looking to expand their research portfolio; to public and private organizations seeking to fulfill their diversity goals by broadening participation to include talent that has been historically underutilized; and to individuals desiring to add value to their personal lives, to the organizations they serve, and ultimately to the global community. Early in his federal career, Dr. Shepard provided definitive data showing the role a small cadre of these institutions can play in conducting high-quality research. In 1984, he was in the Office of Research at the U.S. Nuclear Regulatory Commission (NRC) when he successfully secured joint funding from inside the agency to create NRC's first HBCU research support program. That same year, NRC granted him a leave of absence under the Intergovernmental Personnel Assistance (IPA) program to become a visiting research scientist in the Department of Chemistry at Howard University. He used his IPA assignment to develop a conceptual framework demonstrating how collaborations and partnerships could be used to strengthen the research infrastructure at HBCUs, resulting in more research output by these institutions. At the end of his IPA assignment in 1988, he returned to NRC. In 1990, he resigned from NRC to lead the formation of a university, government, and federal laboratory 501(c)(3), nonprofit partnership called the Science and Engineering Alliance, Inc. (known as SEA). Dr. Shepard earned a B.S. degree in chemistry from Saint Augustine's College (now University) in 1969, and M.S. and Ph.D. degrees in chemistry from Howard University in 1971 and 1973, respectively. His specialty at the graduate level was physical organic chemistry with a focus on mass spectroscopy. In addition to the United States, Dr. Shepard has traveled internationally to engage in research collaborations and present his work in Scotland, England, France, Germany, Austria, Italy, China, and Africa. He serves on several advisory boards, a member of various societies and organizations, a past Sigma Xi Distinguished Lecturer and has received numerous awards and honors including the 21st Century Trailblazer Award from the City Council of Jackson Mississippi. He is a member of Alpha Phi Alpha fraternity.

Aaron Wecksler, Ph.D. – Genentech

Aaron Wecksler is a technical development senior scientist at Genentech. He is a protein biochemist with expertise in analytical characterization of therapeutic antibodies, preclinical small molecule anticancer therapeutics, and protein structure-function relationships. He is responsible for the assay development and characterization of therapeutic antibodies, analytical lead for early-/late-stage biotherapeutics, and the technical development lead of footprinting-mass spectrometry technologies for protein structural analysis. He has a strong interest in the development of young scientists as reflected by being a standing mentor for multiple programs, including the Pharma Technical Development Postdoctoral Program and Process Development Rotational Program (PDRP). Dr. Wecksler was a National Institutes of Health postdoctoral fellow at the University of California, Davis. He has a Ph.D. in chemistry and biochemistry from the University of California, Santa Cruz, where he also received his B.S. in biochemistry and molecular biology.

TUESDAY, MAY 23, 2023 (MST)
10:00–11:30 Institutional Challenges to Developing Partnerships

Moderator:

Abigail S. Newsome, Ph.D. – Mississippi Valley State University

Abigail S. Newsome, a native of Itta Bena, Mississippi, attended Leflore County High School. After her graduation, she studied biology at Mississippi Valley State University (MVSU) and later attended the University of Southern Mississippi where she obtained her Ph.D. in biology with a concentration in molecular biology. She then began her professional tenure at Mississippi Valley State University in August of 1997, where she began teaching biology and microbiology in the Department of Natural Sciences and Environmental Health. During this time, she worked closely with the MVSU Football Team serving as film/video coordinator. Dr. Newsome has also served as a visiting professor of biology at the University of the Virgin Islands in St. Thomas, U.S. Virgin Islands, and has engaged in various collaborations and partnerships at universities across the country and abroad. Dr. Newsome presently serves as Mississippi Valley State University's faculty athletics representative. Her academic position at MVSU is the director of bioinformatics where her efforts are focused on graduate education and research in genomics. Dr. Newsome and her husband, Dr. Albert L. Love, have three adult children and two grandsons.

Panelists:

Ganesh C. Bora, Ph.D. – Fayetteville State University

Ganesh C. Bora is Fayetteville State University's associate vice chancellor for research and innovation, effective August 1, 2022. Previously, Dr. Bora was with the U.S. Department of Agriculture (USDA), where he served as the national program leader of data science and biological engineering at USDA's National Institute of Food and Agriculture (NIFA). NIFA is the grant-funding agency of the USDA, where he led Urban, Indoor, and Emerging Agriculture; Regional Innovation and Climate Smart Agriculture for Future Farms; Farm of the Future; National Robotics Initiative; and Artificial Intelligence Research Institutes and Data Science for Food and Agricultural Systems programs. Dr. Bora represented the USDA in the Networking and Information Technology Research and Development Program of the National Science and Technology Council of the White House. Prior to that he served as a tenured faculty member at Mississippi State University and North Dakota State University. He collaborated on projects with nine countries in Asia, Europe, and Africa. He earned his Ph.D. in biological and agricultural engineering from Kansas State University in Manhattan, Kansas. He is active in professional pursuits and is an engineering program evaluator for the Accreditation Board for Engineering and Technology, Inc. He has been an active member of the American Society of Agricultural and Biological Engineers for 20 years and chaired the Executive Committee on Global Engagement. Dr. Bora is also a U.S. expert on smart farming and agricultural machinery in the International Organization for Standardization.

Elmer Guy, Ph.D. – Navajo Technical University

Since 2006, Elmer Guy has served as the president of Navajo Technical University (NTU), which is a member of the American Indian Higher Education Consortium, a community of 37 tribally and federally chartered institutions of higher education. Navajo Technical University offers certificate to master's degree programs. Prior to becoming president, Dr. Guy also served NTU as its vice president of academics and student services and its dean of instruction. In 2011 and 2012, under Dr. Guy's leadership, NTU was named one of the top 120 community colleges in the United States by the Aspen Institute's College Excellence Program. Before joining NTU, he was appointed by the Navajo Nation president to serve as both the executive director and deputy director of the Navajo Nation Department of Education. During his tenure with the Navajo Nation Department of Education, several needed programs were successfully developed and implemented, including two trusts for people with disabilities ($7 million) and for vocational education programs ($6 million); the Navajo Medicine Man Apprentice School; and a comprehensive teacher education program, all of which have been institutionalized and remain in full operation. Dr. Guy earned his undergraduate and doctorate degrees from the University of Arizona, and in between, a graduate degree from the University of San Francisco. Dr. Guy serves on the board of the American Indian Higher Education Consortium, the American Indian College Fund Board, the College Board's Community Colleges Advisory Panel, as well as other regional and national associations.

Teresa Merriweather Orok, Ph.D. – Alabama A&M University

Teresa Merriweather Orok is an expert on economic and business innovation. While her career spans more than 30 years of experience across grants, government contract management, economic development, government, and higher education, she currently serves as the inaugural director of the Center for Entrepreneurship, Innovation and Economic Development at Alabama A&M University. She assisted more than 200 businesses in start-up and business scaling, including her work with more than 75 businesses across the state of Alabama to aid in COVID-19 pandemic revitalization and stabilization. In addition to her work with statewide and regional incubating start-ups, growing small businesses, and managing large-scale business and government partnerships, Dr. Orok also facilitates student education around entrepreneurship and innovation skills to best prepare students at Historically Black Colleges and Universities for the future of work.

Sheryl H. Ehrman, Ph.D., P.E. – San José State University

Sheryl Ehrman has served as the Don Beall Dean of the College of Engineering at San José State University since 2017. As dean, she oversees 26 academic programs, delivered by 290 faculty and instructors, that serve more than 6,500 students, as well as the College of Engineering's growing research enterprise. She has cultivated strong relationships between the university and Silicon Valley companies, hired award-winning engineering faculty, and established new speaker series and career-prep incentive programs for the college's students. On her watch, the percentage of female engineering professors has grown to one of the highest in the country. Before her current role, Dean Ehrman served as Keystone professor and chair of the Department of Chemical and Biomolecular Engineering at the University of Maryland, College Park. She is a licensed professional engineer in the state of Maryland. Dean Ehrman has a Ph.D. in chemical engineering (aerosol science and technology with a minor in atmospheric science) from the University of California, Los Angeles, and a B.S. in chemical engineering from the University of California, Santa Barbara. Dean Ehrman served as a visiting scientist with the National Institute of Standards and Technology in Maryland and as a National Science Foundation–sponsored postdoctoral fellow at the Paul Scherrer Institute in Switzerland. In 2006, she was named a Fulbright Scholar and visiting associate professor at the Indian Institute of Technology Bombay, where she engaged with students and faculty in the Department of Chemical Engineering. She served as a Fulbright Alumni Ambassador from 2013 to 2016.

11:40–12:20 Applied Research Institute for Mathematics and Computational Sciences

Chad Womack, Ph.D. – United Negro College Fund

Chad Womack is the senior director of National STEM Programs and Initiatives. Prior to joining the United Negro College Fund (UNCF), Dr. Womack co-founded the America21 Project and DC Innovates, both innovation-based community and economic development nonprofit organizations dedicated to empowering metro-centers and underserved communities through STEM education, tech-entrepreneurship, and access to capital. In addition, Dr. Womack led the White House–based Historically Black Colleges and Universities (HBCU) Startup and Innovation Initiative, which resulted in the launch of the HBCU Innovation, Commercialization and Entrepreneurship initiative at UNCF. At UNCF, Dr. Womack's work portfolio includes the Fund II Foundation STEM Scholars Program—a $50 million and 10-year commitment to support 500 academically talented African American high school students pursuing STEM as majors in college and careers in the technology industry; the Ernest E. Just Life Sciences Institute, which includes the Bristol-Myers Squibb–sponsored EE Just Life Sciences Postgraduate Fellowship Program; the UNCF HBCU Innovation, Commercialization and Entrepreneurship Initiative; the UNCF HBCU Innovation Summit and the HBCU Center of Excellence in Computing and Computer Science, which includes a partnership with Google. Dr. Womack was previously a member of the U.S. Department of Commerce, Economic Development Agency, National Advisory Council for Innovation and Entrepreneurship, and the D.C. Mayor's Innovation and Technology

Inclusion Council. Dr. Womack completed several postdoctoral research fellowships at the National Institutes of Health in the National Institutes for Allergy and Infectious Diseases Vaccine Research Center, and at the Harvard AIDS Institute and the Harvard School of Public Health in the Department of Immunology and Infectious Diseases. Dr. Womack earned his doctoral degree in biomedical sciences from the Morehouse School of Medicine and is a proud graduate of Morehouse College, where he majored in biology with minors in chemistry and applied physics.

12:30–1:30 Federal Partnership Programs

Moderator:

Keith A. McGee, Ph.D. – Alcorn State University

Keith A. McGee, a native of Quitman, located in Clarke County, Mississippi, began his postsecondary education at Mississippi Valley State University, majoring in biology and culminating with a Ph.D. from the University of Southern Mississippi in molecular biology. Dr. McGee's research focused on a family of ATP (adenosine triphosphate) transport proteins, specifically those involved in phenotypic multidrug resistance. As a faculty member, he sustained a productive graduate student training program, advising many master's degree–seeking students, along with many undergraduates, and summer research students. Dr. McGee has served in multiple administrative capacities at Alcorn State University; most recently he was appointed to serve as the inaugural associate provost for research, innovation, and graduate education. In this role, Dr. McGee is responsible for providing leadership in developing a clear research vision and growing the university's research footprint while leading and elevating the university's interdisciplinary research activities. Dr. McGee is charged with promoting an understanding and drive for new research opportunities, working with the university deans on all aspects of research and graduate education to ensure alignment with their specific disciplines, while supporting and expanding innovative graduate programs and scholarly activity.

Panelists:

Jesus V. Soriano Molla, Ph.D. – National Science Foundation

Jesus V. Soriano Molla, Ph.D., is a program director at the National Science Foundation (NSF) for the Small Business Innovation Research (SBIR) and Small Business Technology Transfer (STTR) programs. SBIR and STTR are highly competitive programs that encourage domestic small businesses to engage in federal research/research and development (R/R&D) with the potential for commercialization. Through a competitive awards-based program, SBIR and STTR enable small businesses to explore their technological potential and provide the incentive to profit from its commercialization. By including qualified small businesses in the nation's R&D arena, high-tech innovation is stimulated, and the United States gains entrepreneurial spirit as it meets its specific research and development needs. Central to the STTR program is the partnership between small businesses and nonprofit research institutions. The STTR program requires the small business to formally collaborate with a research institution in Phase I and Phase II. STTR's most important role is to bridge the gap between performance of basic science and commercialization of resulting innovations. Previously, Dr. Soriano served as SBIR/STTR program director for biomedical and smart health technologies. He joined NSF after 20 years of leadership experience across industry, nonprofit, and academic sectors. Prior to NSF, he was the senior advisor to the Puerto Rico Trust for Science, Technology and Research. Before that, he was executive vice president at QRxPharma, Ltd., senior director of business development at Osiris Therapeutics, Inc., held several executive leadership positions at ATCC (American Type Culture Collection), and was associate director for R&D operations and business development at Entremed, Inc. Dr. Soriano began his career as a family doctor in Spain, then worked at the University of Geneva Medical School as a research scientist and assistant professor. He came to the United States as a visiting scientist to the National Cancer Institute. He holds an M.B.A. from the Johns Hopkins Carey Business School, a Ph.D. in medical sciences from the University of Geneva, and an M.D. from the University of Alicante, Spain.

Terrence Mosley – Department of Energy

Terrence Mosley is one of the Office of Energy Efficiency and Renewable Energy's leaders in ensuring diversity, equity, and inclusion are woven into EERE (Energy Efficiency and Renewable Energy) activities, programs, and engagement. As senior advisor for diversity, Mr. Mosley is focused on ensuring broad diversity in STEM development, engagement, and recruitment programs. Based in his native Jackson, Mississippi, he brings an extensive knowledge of the STEM field, having earned a B.S. in mechanical engineering at Southern University and A&M College, a historically Black university in Louisiana, and an M.S. in mechanical engineering at the Georgia Institute of Technology. He worked in the automotive industry for nearly two decades in various engineering and management roles with industry leaders such as General Motors and Delphi Packard Electric Systems.

One of Mr. Mosley's proudest STEM outreach accomplishments occurred during his time at Delphi, when he served as the executive sponsor for a new Jackson Public School FIRST Robotics Competition team. A group of volunteers turned the team into multiple-award winners at the regional and national levels over 10 years. He then pivoted his career to entrepreneurship and became the president of a small construction firm that redeveloped foreclosed properties into affordable homes, before he joined the U.S. Department of Energy (DOE). His DOE journey began in 2019 when he became a Science and Technology Policy fellow at the American Association for the Advancement of Science. His background in construction and engineering made him a perfect match for the work under way in EERE's Building Technologies Office. There, he tackled initiatives focused on diversifying the pipeline of the STEM workforce, particularly in the sustainability and efficiency fields. Today, Mr. Mosley is expanding on this work across all EERE's program areas.

Some initiatives and collaborations Mr. Mosley works on include the Minority-Serving Institutions STEM Research and Development Consortium, a consortium of more than 70 Minority-Serving Institutions that promote innovative research and development in the clean energy space. The program has active projects focused on building technologies and solar power, with potential projects in bioenergy, water, and wind power. Another initiative is the Graduate Education for Minority Students Fellowship, which recruits underrepresented students seeking graduate degrees in applied science and STEM fields. Moving forward, much of Mr. Mosley's focus is on partnering with other government agencies, such as the National Science Foundation, to pool efforts and connect talented people in underrepresented groups with a range of STEM programs that EERE has to offer.

Final Workshop – Building Defense Research Capacity at HBCUs, TCUs, HSIs and ANNHSIs (June 28–29, 2023)
Chicago, Illinois (Hybrid)

WEDNESDAY, JUNE 28, 2023
9:00 – 9:05 Opening Remarks

Moderator:

Oscar Barton, Jr., Ph.D., P.E. – Morgan State University

Oscar Barton, Jr., is a professor and dean of the Morgan State University Clarence M. Mitchell, Jr. School of Engineering. A native of Washington, DC, he received his B.S. in mechanical engineering from Tuskegee (Institute) University, and his M.S. in mechanical engineering, and Ph.D. in applied mechanics from Howard University in 1993. He joined Morgan in fall 2020, after completing 6 years at George Mason University (GMU) and a 22-year career at the U.S. Naval Academy. Dr. Barton's research focuses on the development of approximate closed form solutions for linear self-adjoint systems, those that govern the responses of composite structures, and the analysis of dynamic systems. More recently, he investigated the dynamic response of flexible composite structures subject to periodic and random excitation. He has mentored numerous midshipmen through independent research projects and has directed two Trident Scholars, the Naval Academy's flagship research program. He has published more than 60 journal and conference articles on these topics.

While at the Naval Academy and in its 163-year history, Dr. Barton was one of only three African Americans to obtain the rank of tenured full professor and the first to achieve this milestone in the Division of Engineering and Weapons, Division I. In 2010, he assumed the role of chairman of the mechanical engineering department, responsible for its strategic leadership and planning of its faculty, midshipmen-student body, curriculum, and resources. During his time as chair, the department revived and accredited the General Engineering program and created the Nuclear Engineering program, the first ever offering at the academy. Dr. Barton chaired the largest department in the Division I consisting of 42 civilian and military faculty professionals, and promoted a vibrant research and academic environment in energy and propulsion, nuclear energy, structures and materials, and design. As the founding department chair at GMU, Dr. Barton ushered growth of the department from 3 faculty and 12 students to 17 faculty and 385 undergraduate students and 6 doctoral students as of spring 2020.

Under his leadership the undergraduate program received initial EAC-ABET (Engineering Accreditation Commission–Accreditation Board for Engineering and Technology accreditation retroactive to fall 2015, and was reaccredited to fall 2024, established state-of-the-art teaching and research labs on GMU's Sci-Tech campus, and authored an interim Ph.D. program, which is in its final stages of seeking approval from the State Council of Final Higher Education for Virginia.

A fellow of the American Society of Mechanical Engineers (ASME), Dr. Barton is actively involved in academic innovations and program assessment. He chairs ASME's Committee on Engineering Education, is a member of the ASME Public Affairs and Outreach Council, and is a member-at-large on the Engineering Accreditation Commission's Executive Committee of ABET, after having served numerous years as a program evaluator and commissioner. He is a registered engineer licensed to practice engineering in the state of Maryland.

9:05 – 10:00 Transitioning from Low to High Research Activity

Moderator:

Thomas Tubon, Ph.D. – BioMADE

Thomas Tubon is the chief workforce development officer for BioMADE. Prior to his appointment with BioMADE, he served as a professor in the Biotechnology Program at Madison Area Technical College for 13 years. During this time, he led several National Science Foundation (NSF) Advanced Technological Education initiatives to establish and scale an emerging technology program in stem cells and cell manufacturing and directed a National Coordination Network in Advanced Manufacturing of Cell and Tissue Products. While at Madison College, Dr. Tubon was responsible for the development of bioscience workforce and strategic implementation of programs for local-, regional-, and national-level adoption and scale-up. In this role, he has facilitated the creation of a broad network of industry, community, and academic stakeholders designed to foster career pathways in STEM. He also serves as a mentor with the NSF Advanced Technological Education (ATE) Mentor Connect and Project Vision Programs. Dr. Tubon held leadership roles with the NSF ATE InnovATEBIO Center for Biotechnology Education, and the NSF Advancing Research Impact in Society Center with a focus on education, workforce development, and strategic partnerships. Dr. Tubon holds a Ph.D. in molecular genetics from Stony Brook University and Cold Spring Harbor Laboratory and a B.S. in molecular biology from San Diego State University.

Panelists:

Rosemarie D. Wesson, Ph.D. –City College of New York

Rosemarie D. Wesson recently joined the Grove School of Engineering at the City College of New York as the associated dean for research in August 2015 and brings a broad knowledge of diverse engineering fields to the school. Dr. Wesson has more than 13 years of experience at the National Science Foundation (NSF) in the Directorate for Engineering and excelled as both a director and program director. As acting director of the Emerging Frontiers in Research and Innovation (EFRI) Office, Dr. Wesson was a member of the Engineering Leadership Team and led the EFRI office. As a program director at NSF, she managed both small-business and academic research portfolios focused on energy, nanotechnology, emerging research opportunities, and the field of chemical and biological separations. Dr. Wesson received the NSF Director's Award for Collaborative Integration and the Director's Award for Superior Accomplishment. Prior to NSF, Dr. Wesson was a faculty member in the Department of Chemical Engineering at Louisiana State University in Baton Rouge, Louisiana.

Dr. Wesson has authored or co-authored numerous technical papers in the area of numerical analyses of polymer crystallization kinetics, structure-property relationships of crystalline materials, and finite-element analyses of polymeric flows. She was awarded both outstanding teaching and research awards at Louisiana State University. In industry, Dr. Wesson worked as a senior research leader in the Corporate Materials Science Research and Development Lab of Dow Chemical Company. Her responsibilities included supervision and leadership in the polymer rheology research arena. She led multiple teams of researchers in bench level, miniplant, pilot plant, and production facilities resulting in significant cost savings for the company. Dr. Wesson has also led nonprofit research. As a principal researcher at the Battelle Memorial Institute, she led a team to research and manufacture the Odyssey Atlasphere, which received an R&D 100 Award for one of the 100 most technologically significant new products of the year. She is a fellow in the American Institute of Chemical Engineers (AIChE). She has held numerous leadership positions within AIChE. She recently ended a 3-year term on the AIChE Board of Directors and received the 2014 Minority Action Committee Eminent Chemical Engineers Award for outstanding contributions to the minority chemical engineering community. She is a member of the American Chemical

Society and the American Society for Engineering Education (ASEE). Dr. Wesson is also an invited contributing author for the ASEE *PRISM* magazine. The quarterly Discovery articles highlight timely and relevant engineering discoveries for national and international audiences. Dr. Wesson received her B.S. in chemical engineering from the Massachusetts Institute of Technology, and her M.S. and Ph.D., both in chemical engineering, from the University of Michigan. Dr. Wesson is a registered professional engineer.

Gillian Wilson, Ph.D. – University of California, Merced

Gillian Wilson is vice chancellor for research, innovation, and economic development at the University of California (UC), Merced. She previously served as a senior associate vice chancellor for research and economic development and as professor of physics and astronomy at UC Riverside. During her tenure at UC Riverside, Dr. Wilson's administrative experience included serving as interim deputy director of the University of California Observatories, UC Riverside director of the California Institute for Telecommunications and Information Technology, interim divisional dean for physical sciences and mathematics, and chair of the College of Natural and Agricultural Sciences Executive Committee. Dr. Wilson's research expertise is in observational cosmology and galaxy evolution. She leads several large international astronomy collaborations, and her work has resulted in more than 110 refereed publications and more than $10 million in extramural funding and telescope time. She is committed to public outreach and, especially, to attracting women and minorities into the STEM fields. Her outreach activities have touched more than 50,000 people. Dr. Wilson holds a Ph.D. in physics from the University of Durham and a B.Sc. in physics from the University of Glasgow. She is a fellow of the American Physical Society and the American Astronomical Society.

10:00 – 11:00 Recruiting Research-Centered Faculty at Non-R1 institutions

Moderator:

Chad Womack, Ph.D. – United Negro College Fund

Chad Womack is the senior director of National STEM Programs and Initiatives. Prior to joining the United Negro College Fund (UNCF), Dr. Womack co-founded the America21 Project and DC Innovates, both innovation-based community and economic development nonprofit organizations dedicated to empowering metro-centers and underserved communities through STEM education, tech-entrepreneurship, and access to capital. In addition, Dr. Womack led the White House–based Historically Black Colleges and Universities (HBCU) Startup and Innovation Initiative, which resulted in the launch of the HBCU Innovation, Commercialization and Entrepreneurship initiative at UNCF. At UNCF, Dr. Womack's work portfolio includes the Fund II Foundation STEM Scholars Program—a $50 million and 10-year commitment to support 500 academically talented African American high school students pursuing STEM as majors in college and careers in the technology industry; the Ernest E. Just Life Sciences Institute, which includes the Bristol-Myers Squibb–sponsored EE Just Life Sciences Postgraduate Fellowship Program; the UNCF HBCU Innovation, Commercialization and Entrepreneurship Initiative; the UNCF HBCU Innovation Summit and the HBCU Center of Excellence in Computing and Computer Science, which includes a partnership with Google. Dr. Womack was previously a member of the U.S. Department of Commerce, Economic Development Agency, National Advisory Council for Innovation and Entrepreneurship, and the D.C. Mayor's Innovation and Technology Inclusion Council. Dr. Womack completed several postdoctoral research fellowships at the National Institutes of Health in the National Institutes for Allergy and Infectious Diseases Vaccine Research Center, and at the Harvard AIDS Institute and the Harvard School of Public Health in the Department of Immunology and Infectious Diseases. Dr. Womack earned his doctoral degree in biomedical sciences from the Morehouse School of Medicine and is a proud graduate of Morehouse College, where he majored in biology with minors in chemistry and applied physics.

Panelists:

Joanna Brooks, Ph.D. – San Diego State University

Joanna Brooks is an award-winning author or editor of 10 books on race, religion, gender, social movements, and American culture. She has appeared in global media outlets, including the BBC, NPR, the *Daily Show*, CNN, MSNBC, and the *Washington Post*. In her role as associate vice president for faculty advancement and student success at San Diego State University (SDSU), she leads faculty development and student academic support efforts. Dr. Brooks is a graduate of the California State University Executive Leadership program and a founder of SDSU's Digital Humanities Center and Shared Governance Leadership Institute. She joined the SDSU faculty in 2006 as an associate professor of English and comparative literature and has served as department chair and associate dean of graduate and research affairs. She holds a Ph.D. in English from the University of California, Los Angeles.

Catherine K. Armwood-Gordon, Ph.D. – Tennessee State University

Catherine K. Armwood-Gordon is currently associate professor in the Department of Civil and Architectural Engineering at Tennessee State University (TSU). She received her Ph.D. in architectural engineering from the University of Nebraska–Lincoln (2014) and a B.S. in architectural engineering from Tennessee State University (2007). Her technical expertise is structural engineering, with research interest in the study of the behavior of structural materials and structural performance of existing structures and structures subjected to natural disasters. She also conducts research in faculty development and engineering education. She is the director of student services and outreach for the College of Engineering. She holds the positions of TSU regional director for the Tennessee Science Olympiad; TSU National Summer Transportation Institute director; board member of the Nashville Region Architecture, Construction, and Engineering Organization; treasurer of the Music City Professionals of the National Society of Black Engineers; and serves on the Metro Public Schools STEM Advisory Board and Tennessee Department of Education STEM Advisory Council.

Ivan Mosley, Ph.D. – Tennessee State University

Ivan Mosley is the chair of the Department of Applied and Industrial Technologies at Tennessee State University. He was born in Winston-Salem, North Carolina, and attended the public schools of the city. In high school, he received vocational training along with completing a general education core curriculum. After high school, he attended North Carolina Agricultural & Technical State University (NCA&TSU) and participated on the university's cross-country and track team. At NCA&TSU, a few dedicated professors, staff, and family members embraced him to graduate with a degree in manufacturing systems. Upon graduating from NCA&TSU, his first professional employment was with the North Carolina Army National Guard as a platoon leader, 731st Maintenance Company in Reidsville, North Carolina. While on active duty, he completed the requirements for a master's degree in information science at North Carolina Central University as well as a second master's from the University of Central Missouri in Warrensburg, Missouri, and was once again embraced by caring faculty, staff, and family members who influenced the pursuit of a Ph.D. at the Ohio State University. At Ohio State, dedicated faculty, staff, family, and mentors enabled Dr. Mosley to become a strong professional in higher education. Over the past 20 years, he has been afforded opportunities to work with governmental agencies, higher education institutions, industry, and the military with online curriculum development, manufacturing strategic planning, accreditation, and technology integration through STEM initiatives.

11:10 – 12:10 Adapting Administrative Bandwidth for Increased Research Activity

Moderator:

Abraham Wolcott, Ph.D. – San José State University

Abraham Wolcott is a physical chemist who focuses on the surface chemistry of nanoscale and bulk materials for biological labeling and alternative energy production (solar cell research). He received a B.S. and Ph.D. with Professor Jin Z. Zhang at the University of California, Santa Cruz (Jin Zhang group). He received a National Science Foundation postdoctoral fellowship and worked with Professor Xiao Yang Zhu at the University of Texas at Austin, who then moved to Columbia University. He also worked with Profs. Jon Owen at Columbia and Dirk Englund at the Massachusetts Institute of Technology as a joint postdoctoral scientist before moving to San José State University. Prof. Wolcott has taught physical chemistry lectures (Chem 160) and laboratory (Chem 162L) and has received several grants to incorporate technology into the physical chemistry course curriculum. One pedagogical tool that is being incorporated is the use of virtual reality (VR) in the classroom. Thermodynamics, chemical kinetics, quantum mechanics, and spectroscopy are topics in which VR-based lesson plans can be developed.

Panelists:

Almesha L. Campbell, Ph.D. – Jackson State University

Almesha L. Campbell serves as the assistant vice president for research and economic development/director for technology transfer and commercialization at Jackson State University (JSU). She provides support for the overall direction of the Division of Research and Economic Development and manages the intellectual property process from triage of invention disclosures to commercialization. She provides strategic direction and vision for defining partnerships in research, commercialization, entrepreneurship, and innovation initiatives between JSU and other institutions, funding agencies, and industry stakeholders. Dr. Campbell is the principal investigator for the

National Science Foundation–funded JSU Innovation Corps Site designed to train teams of faculty and students how to commercialize their ideas using the Lean Startup Methodology. She also leads several initiatives geared toward increasing the innovation, technology transfer, invention, and entrepreneurial activities at JSU, such as the JSU Center for Innovation and Entrepreneurship, which houses the XR Academy, Makerspace, and Learning Collaboratory. Dr. Campbell received her bachelor's degree from the University of Central Florida, and her master's degree in mass communications and doctor of philosophy degree in public policy and administration from Jackson State University. She holds membership in professional organizations such as the Licensing Executives Society, the Association of University Technology Managers, and the American Society of Public Administration.

Laura Collins, Ph.D. – North Carolina Agricultural and Technical State University

Laura Collins is director of intellectual property development and commercialization at North Carolina Agricultural and Technical State University (N.C. A&T). Dr. Collins also served as the licensed patent agent for N.C. A&T and as the intellectual property liaison between the vice chancellor for the Division of Research and Economic Development, or DORED, and agencies, businesses, and law firms hired for patent prosecution and licensing. She is responsible for reviewing all requests for patent licensing about protection of the university's intellectual property. She evaluates submissions of preliminary ideas and invention disclosures to determine the feasibility of filing for patents on behalf of principal investigators and the university. She also works with faculty to evaluate the innovative merit of proposed research programs. Before joining the Office of Outreach and Economic Development in 2010, she spent 10 years with intellectual property law firms. As a patent agent and scientific advisor, she prosecuted foreign and domestic patent applications on topics including radiolabeled antibodies, small molecule and biotech therapeutics, microfluidic devices, activated carbons used in electric double layer capacitors, and silicon inks used in printed electronics. She also conducted inventorship investigations, as well as freedom-to-operate and prior art landscape analyses. She is registered to practice before the U.S. Patent and Trademark Office and is a member of the American Chemical Society. She has undergraduate degrees in chemistry, with honors, and history from Bryn Mawr College, and a Ph.D. in chemistry from the University of North Carolina at Chapel Hill.

Elmer Guy, Ph.D. – Navajo Technical University

Since 2006, Elmer Guy has served as the president of Navajo Technical University (NTU), which is a member of the American Indian Higher Education Consortium, a community of 37 tribally and federally chartered institutions of higher education. Navajo Technical University offers certificate to master's degree programs. Prior to becoming president, Dr. Guy also served NTU as its vice president of academics and student services and its dean of instruction. In 2011 and 2012, under Dr. Guy's leadership, NTU was named one of the top 120 community colleges in the United States by the Aspen Institute's College Excellence Program. Before joining NTU, he was appointed by the Navajo Nation president to serve as both the executive director and deputy director of the Navajo Nation Department of Education. During his tenure with the Navajo Nation Department of Education, several needed programs were successfully developed and implemented, including two trusts for people with disabilities ($7 million) and for vocational education programs ($6 million); the Navajo Medicine Man Apprentice School; and a comprehensive teacher education program, all of which have been institutionalized and remain in full operation. Dr. Guy earned his undergraduate and doctorate degrees from the University of Arizona, and in between, a graduate degree from the University of San Francisco. Dr. Guy serves on the board of the American Indian Higher Education Consortium, the American Indian College Fund Board, the College Board's Community Colleges Advisory Panel, as well as other regional and national associations.

THURSDAY, JUNE 29, 2023 (CDT)
10:00 – 11:00 Barriers to Expanding the Defense Research Workforce Pipeline

Moderator:

Bryn L. Adams, Ph.D. – U.S. Army DEVCOM Army Research Laboratory

Bryn L. Adams received a B.S. in biology in 2001 and a Ph.D. in interdisciplinary biology in 2009 from the University of North Carolina at Charlotte. Her doctoral studies included a variety of research projects in the field of applied and environmental microbiology. Dr. Adams completed two postdoctoral fellowships; the first was a collaborative project, as a National Academy of Sciences postdoctoral fellow, between DEVCOM Chemical Biological Center and the Institute of Bioscience and Biotechnology Research at the University of Maryland, College Park, which focused on the development of nonspecific threat agent detection using simple biological sensing and signal transduction pathways. The second fellowship was with DEVCOM Army Research Laboratory as an Oak Ridge Associated Universities postdoctoral fellow, where she conducted research into the development of synthetic molecular recognition agents for biosensing and biomaterials. In 2014, Dr. Adams converted to a federal civilian research scientist at the Army Research Lab. She has led the Synbio Tools and Chassis Team in the Biotechnology Branch since 2018. Her research efforts currently focus on developing synthetic biology tools for nonmodel host bacteria and establishing the capability of synthetic biology from the lab and into the hands of the warfighter. She has published more than 20 peer-reviewed manuscripts on a wide range of bacterial biotechnology topics across several disciplines and was awarded the Department of Defense (DOD) Scientist of the Quarter in 2019 for her contributions to the field of biotechnology for DOD. Dr. Adams is currently on a 1-year detail assignment to the Office of the Under Secretary of Defense for Research and Engineering, where she leads the Education and Workforce Development component of the Biotechnology Modernization Priority.

Panelists:

Shannon Arnold, M.Eng., M.S. – Office of the Under Secretary of Defense for Research and Engineering

Shannon Arnold is a Principle Scientist at GBL Systems Corporation. Mr. Arnold is a prolific engineer with over 30 years of experience working in government and industry serving as research and development engineering in organizations such as the National Aeronautics and Space Administration and the Scientific Research Corporation. His work and passion has also included identifying opportunities to broaden defense-related research and development opportunities for individuals from underrepresented communities. Mr. Arnold earned a B.S. in chemistry and mathematics from Morehouse College in 1992, a M.S. in organic and polymer chemistry from Clark Atlanta University in 1994, and a M.Eng. from Virginia Tech in 1998.

Kerin Hilker-Balkissoon, Ph.D. – George Mason University

Kerin Hilker-Balkissoon brings more than 20 years of experience engaging PK–12, community college, university, nonprofit, and workforce sectors to address systemic inequities and barriers to college access, success, and career attainment. Her innovative efforts are grounded in justice, equity, diversity, and inclusion, integrating career pathways; high-impact educational practices; asset-based approaches; and developmental, holistic student supports. A NISTS (National Institute for the Study of Transfer Students) Transfer Champion-Catalyst award winner, Dr. Hilker-Balkissoon has a proven track record in designing data-driven interventions that enhance postsecondary inclusive excellence for underserved and minoritized groups. She specializes in supporting community college and transfer students, student-parents, first-generation students, immigrant and international students, and posttraditional (adult) populations. At George Mason University (GMU), she designs and implements College of Science pathways that enhance STEM access and success, and teaches in the Scientific Leadership and Practice program. She actively engages in university-wide efforts to enhance inclusive excellence, including service as co-chair of the Student-Parent Task Force, tri-chair to GMU's First-Generation Task Force, the Undocumented Student Task Force, and the Transfer Advisory Council. Herself a first-generation Latina college graduate, she actively gives her time to advocacy and support of the Hispanic and Autistic communities, including a leadership role with nonprofit Friends in Need Virginia, and as a board member for the Virginia Latino Higher Education Network.

Charlene Mello, Ph.D. – University of Massachusetts Dartmouth

Charlene Mello has 33 years of experience in research, development, and engineering in both government and academia. She obtained her Ph.D. from the University of Massachusetts Lowell in chemistry under the supervision of Professor Kenneth Marx. She has co-authored more than 100 peer-reviewed publications and 14 patents. Her technical experience encompasses technical areas such as protein self-assembly, biomaterials, biosensing, and the bio-abio interface. She has participated in numerous organizing committees for national and international scientific meetings, was a member of the Biotechnology Team of Experts for NATO Land Group 7 and scientific advisor for the National Research Council Postdoctoral Fellowship Program, and has held academic appointments at the Massachusetts Institute of Technology and the University of Massachusetts. Prior to departing from government service, she served as the Army DEVCOM Soldier Center chief scientist, where her responsibilities were to oversee the execution of science and technology programs and execution of the Soldier Center Basic Research program. Together with other technical leaders in the Army, she co-authored the Army Futures Command, Synthetic Biology Strategy. Her collaborations and outreach with academia facilitated the development of partnerships to provide impactful scientific and technical solutions for soldier protection and performance. Currently, Dr. Mello serves as a STEM mentor and scientific advisor for a Soldier Center National Defense Education Program focused on workforce development in synthetic biology.

11:00 – 12:30 Challenges and Opportunities for Researchers and Personnel Engaging in Federally Funded Research

Moderator:

Oscar Barton, Jr., Ph.D., P.E. – Morgan State University

Oscar Barton, Jr., is a professor and dean of the Morgan State University Clarence M. Mitchell, Jr. School of Engineering. A native of Washington, DC, he received his B.S. in mechanical engineering from Tuskegee (Institute) University, and his M.S. in mechanical engineering and Ph.D. in applied mechanics from Howard University in 1993. Dr. Barton joined Morgan in fall 2020, after completing 6 years at George Mason University (GMU) and a 22-year career at the U.S. Naval Academy. Dr. Barton's research focuses on the development of approximate closed form solutions for linear self-adjoint systems, those that govern the responses of composite structures, and the analysis of dynamic systems. More recently, he investigated the dynamic response of flexible composite structures subject to periodic and random excitation. He has mentored numerous midshipmen through independent research projects and has directed two Trident Scholars, the Naval Academy's flagship research program. He has published more than 60 journal and conference articles on these topics. While at the Naval Academy and in its 163-year history, Dr. Barton was one of only three African Americans to obtain the rank of tenured full professor and the first to achieve this milestone in the Division of Engineering and Weapons, Division I. In 2010, he assumed the role of chairman of the mechanical engineering department, responsible for its strategic leadership and planning of its faculty, midshipmen-student body, curriculum, and resources. During his time as chair, the department revived and accredited the General Engineering program and created the Nuclear Engineering program, the first ever offering at the academy. Dr. Barton chaired the largest department in the Division I consisting of 42 civilian and military faculty professionals, and promoted a vibrant research and academic environment in energy and propulsion, nuclear energy, structures and materials, and design. As the founding department chair at GMU, Dr. Barton ushered growth of the department from 3 faculty and 12 students to 17 faculty and 385 undergraduate students and 6 doctoral students as of spring 2020. Under his leadership, the undergraduate program received initial EAC-ABET (Engineering Accreditation Commission–Accreditation Board for Engineering and Technology) accreditation retroactive to fall 2015, and was reaccredited to fall 2024, established state-of-the-art teaching and research labs on GMU's Sci-Tech campus, and authored an interim Ph.D. program, which is in its final stages of seeking approval from the State Council of Higher Education for Virginia. A fellow of the American Society of Mechanical Engineers (ASME), Dr. Barton is actively involved in academic innovations and program assessment. He chairs ASME's Committee on Engineering Education, is a member of ASME's Public Affairs and Outreach Council, and is a member-at-large on the Engineering Accreditation Commission's Executive Committee of ABET, after having served numerous years as a program evaluator and commissioner. He is a registered engineer licensed to practice engineering in the state of Maryland.

Panelists:

Abraham Wolcott, Ph.D. – San José State University

Abraham Wolcott is a physical chemist who focuses on the surface chemistry of nanoscale and bulk materials for biological labeling and alternative energy production (solar cell research). He received a B.S. and Ph.D. with Professor Jin Z. Zhang at the University of California, Santa Cruz (Jin Zhang group). He received a National Science Foundation postdoctoral fellowship and worked with Professor Xiao Yang Zhu at the University of Texas at Austin, who then moved to Columbia University. He also worked with Profs. Jon Owen at Columbia and Dirk Englund at the Massachusetts Institute of Technology as a joint postdoctoral scientist before moving to San José State University. Prof. Wolcott has taught physical chemistry lectures (Chem 160) and laboratory (Chem 162L) and has received several grants to incorporate technology into the physical chemistry course curriculum. One pedagogical tool that is being incorporated is the use of virtual reality (VR) in the classroom. Thermodynamics, chemical kinetics, quantum mechanics, and spectroscopy are topics in which VR-based lesson plans can be developed.

Saleh Zein-Sabatto, Ph.D. – Tennessee State University

Dr. Zein-Sabatto is the interim department chair and has been a professor in the Department of Electrical and Computer Engineering since

1991. He received his B.S. degree in electric power systems from the University of Aleppo, Syria, in 1979, and M.S. and Ph.D. degrees in electrical engineering from Vanderbilt University in 1986 and 1990, respectively. He worked for industry for 4 years in the area of electric power systems and communication.

Jill Keith, Ph.D. – Winston-Salem State University and Wake Forest University

Jill Keith is a professor of biochemistry and the manager of the Biomedical Research Infrastructure Center at Winston-Salem State University (WSSU) and an adjunct professor in physiology and pharmacology at Wake Forest University. She received a B.S. degree from York College, City University of New York, and a Ph.D. from the University of Maryland, College Park. As a bioorganic chemist with training in pharmacology, she conducts research related to central nervous system diseases and disorders. She served as chair of the Department of Biological Sciences at WSSU and currently teaches in the Department of Chemistry. As such, she uses diverse teaching methods and encourages students to use metacognitive strategies and Bloom's Taxonomy to become self-regulated and life-long learners. In addition, she instructs faculty, staff, and students using the National Science Foundation's I-Corps model and has helped teams develop prototypes that have commercialization potential. Dr. Keith received the Board of Governors Award for Excellence in Teaching for using active learning strategies. She is currently funded to develop molecular probes to study the brain; she also performs research to uncover therapeutics to treat neuronal disorders/diseases. She is the site principal investigator for faculty and student development training grants and has a state contract to help those impacted by COVID-19. She is also funded to instruct faculty on how to teach entrepreneurship to freshmen. Dr. Keith has a history of assisting faculty through her service on WSSU assessment, accreditation, research-related committees, the Internal Review Board, and in facilitating faculty workshops. These collaborative activities have led to faculty promotions, faculty receiving external funding, publications, and several conference presentations. To assist with diversity efforts connected to training the next generation of scientists and health care professionals, Dr. Keith is involved with K–12 outreach activities. As such, she is one of the founders of SciTech which engages K–12 students in hands-on experiments, especially those from historically excluded groups.

Michael Groves, Ph.D. – California State University, Fullerton

Michael Groves is associate professor of physical and theoretical chemistry at California State University, Fullerton. Dr. Groves has authored 20 peer-reviewed publications, contributed to the development of an online education portal, and holds a patent related to the environmentally friendly fabrication of very small chemical reactors. His research program has focused on computationally simulating chemical reactions on surfaces as well as developing the tools necessary to model these surfaces. Some of his other projects include quantifying the role of chirality in hydrogen-carrying fuels for fuel cell applications and the role of physical hole defects in functionalized 2D carbon and boron materials to catalyze electrochemical reactions such as hydrogen peroxide synthesis. Dr. Groves received the prestigious Governor General of Canada's Academic Gold Medal for his doctoral studies and earned his Ph.D. in chemical and material engineering from the Royal Military College of Canada. He holds a master's degree in physics from Queen's University and a bachelor's degree in physics from the University of British Columbia. He is a member of the American Chemical Society.

12:40 – 1:30 Federal Capacity Programs for Faculty and Trainee Support

Moderator:

Keith A. McGee, Ph.D. – Alcorn State University

Keith A. McGee, a native of Quitman, located in Clarke County, Mississippi, began his postsecondary education at Mississippi Valley State University, majoring in biology and culminating with a Ph.D. from the University of Southern Mississippi in molecular biology. Dr. McGee's research focused on a family of ATP (adenosine triphosphate) transport proteins, specifically those involved in phenotypic multidrug resistance. As a faculty member, he sustained a productive graduate student training program, advising many master's degree–seeking students, along with many undergraduates, and summer research students. Dr. McGee has served in multiple administrative capacities at Alcorn State University; most recently he was appointed to serve as the inaugural associate provost for research, innovation, and graduate education. In this role, Dr. McGee is responsible for providing leadership in developing a clear research vision and growing the university's research footprint while leading and elevating the university's interdisciplinary research activities. Dr. McGee is charged with promoting an understanding and drive for new research opportunities, working with the university deans on all aspects of research and graduate education to ensure alignment with their specific disciplines, while supporting and expanding innovative graduate programs and scholarly activity.

Panelists:

Narcrisha S. Norman, Ph.D. – National Science Foundation

Narcrisha S. Norman is a program director at the National Science Foundation (NSF) in the Division of Graduate Education within the Directorate for STEM Education. She contributes to policy within NSF and throughout the federal government with a portfolio of NSF programs that are agency, directorate, and division wide. Her primary focus is the Graduate Research Fellowship Program, the Racial Equity in STEM Education Program (Racial Equity), and the "Dear Colleague Letter: Supplemental Funding for Space-Related Preparation and Awareness for Career Equity (SPACE)." Dr. Norman has a Ph.D. in aerospace engineering and both M.S. and B.S. degrees in mechanical engineering. Prior to NSF, she was an associate professor in engineering. Her research areas include theoretical space physics, general aerodynamics, and postgraduate education. She is committed to supporting continued growth of diversity, equity, inclusion, and accessibility in STEM leadership, research, and education. Dr. Norman encourages participation from the STEM community to serve as NSF reviewers, apply for funding including undergraduate funding, and to request NSF speakers via the NSF Speakers Bureau.

Sailaja Koduri, Ph.D. – National Institutes of Health

Sailaja Koduri is a program director in the Division of Pharmacology, Physiology, and Biological Chemistry at the National Institutes of Health, where she administers a portfolio of research grants in the areas of receptors, drug targets, and signal transduction; adaptive immunity; and SBIR (Small Business Innovation Research) and STTR (Small Business Technology Transfer). She also manages predoctoral training grants in pharmacological sciences and serves as a program contact for the Maximizing Investigators' Research Award for early-stage investigators. Dr. Koduri was formerly a scientific review officer at the National Center for Advancing Translational Sciences, and prior to that she worked as a senior scientist at BioReliance. She earned a B.S. in chemistry from Nagarjuna University and a Ph.D. in biochemistry from the Central Food Technological Research Institute, both in India. Dr. Koduri conducted postdoctoral research at the Howard University College of Medicine and National Cancer Institute.

LaRico Treadwell, Ph.D. – Sandia National Laboratories

LaRico Treadwell is a research and development chemist and material scientist in the Securing Top Academic Research and Talent (START) at Historically Black Colleges and Universities (HBCU) Program at Sandia National Laboratories. He was awarded a 2021 Black Engineer of the Year Award (BEYA) in the category of Most Promising Scientist. BEYA is a program of the national Career Communications Group, an advocate for corporate diversity, and is part of its STEM achievement program. The award recognizes the nation's best and brightest engineers, scientists, and technology experts. Early on in Dr. Treadwell's life, he exhibited a keen intellect with a particular aptitude for science and engineering. He enjoyed taking things apart to see how they worked and experimenting with various foods and household chemicals to see what color/concoction resulted. Everyone, including the immediate family, recognized his inquisitive nature and destined him to be a leader and innovator. He graduated from South Panola High School with honors in 2006 and decided to attend the University of Mississippi (UM) as an Ole Miss First Scholar recipient. Dr. Treadwell was initially interested in pursuing medicine. However, he became a Louis Stokes Mississippi Alliance for Minority–Increasing Minority Access to Graduate Education (LSMAP-IMAGE), Ronald E. McNair, and Alliance for Graduate Education in Mississippi (AGEM) scholar, which introduced him to laboratory research. He worked in the laboratory of Jason Ritchie, associate professor of chemistry, with a focus on hydrogen-powered fuel cells. This experience solidified Dr. Treadwell's commitment to pursuing a B.S. in chemistry degree and going on to graduate school. He became one of the first African Americans to receive a B.S. in chemistry at UM in 2010, as well as the first STEM bachelor's degree of his family. After graduation, Dr. Treadwell enrolled in Louisiana State University (LSU) in the Ph.D. chemistry program as a Board of Regents fellow. He was mentored by Professor Julia Chan in solid state chemistry. Under Dr. Chan's tutelage, he published multiple peer-reviewed articles by developing impressive skills in solid-state chemistry synthesis and with a focus on understanding the physical and chemical behavior of chemical moieties.

While attending LSU, Dr. Treadwell was president of the local chapter of the National Organization for the Professional Advancement of Black Chemists and Chemical Engineers and Chemistry Graduate School Council, among his numerous contributions and participation in local communities through outreach events. In 2015, Dr. Treadwell received his Ph.D. and subsequently accepted a postdoctoral fellow position at Sandia

National Laboratories. As a postdoctoral fellow, Dr. Treadwell studied under Dr. Timothy J. Boyle to master inorganic synthesis of small molecules, fabrication of nanomaterials, and other material processing techniques for a variety of applications, including thermoelectric, circuitry, capacitors, and flywheels. During his tenure as a postdoc, Dr. Treadwell published numerous peer-reviewed journals and filed several patents. In 2017, Dr. Treadwell accepted a position as a research and development chemist at Sandia National Laboratories. He was awarded an Early Career Laboratory Directed Research and Development Award to investigate magneto-inks with an emphasis on increasing materials reliability in engineered devices. His work covers the spectrum from basic materials discovery and characterization through applied materials reliability and device fabrication for a wide range of applications such as radiation, ultra-high-temperature systems, nonlinear optics, and thermoelectrics.

Dr. Treadwell's research advances science frontiers in chemistry, engineering, materials, and component reliability. Additionally, he serves in multiple programmatic roles contributing across the spectrum of nuclear deterrence programs. He serves in leadership roles for materials analysis and compatibility for a wide spectrum of these critical national security programs. Along with his excellent technical work, Dr. Treadwell gives back to the community. He worked with several companies through the New Mexico Small Business Assistance Program. He leads CSI: Dognapping, a highly recognized community outreach program that provides science enrichment for nearly 500 fourth graders every year. Dr. Treadwell was awarded a Sandia Employee Recognition Award for Diversity for championing diversity programs across Sandia, including programs for students from HBCUs into STEM. Overall, Dr. Treadwell's technical success has offered him an opportunity to reach beyond research to impact the development of the next generation of scientists and engineers with a focus on maximizing minority representation in STEM careers.

Helen Turner, Ph.D. – Chaminade University of Honolulu

Dr. Helen Turner serves as professor of biology and faculty in data science at Chaminade University. She is committed to Chaminade's social justice mission and works to advance equity in STEM for minoritized and marginalized individuals, especially low-income, indigenous, and veteran students. As Dean of Natural Sciences and VP for Innovation at Chaminade she led capacity-building efforts in academic excellence and inclusion over a 15-year period, including the establishment of the region's first undergraduate data science major. She was recently appointed Research Director of Chaminade's new United Nations Sustainability Center and is principal investigator of an extensive grant portfolio funded by the National Science Foundation (NSF), National Institutes of Health (NIH), the Department of Defense, and private foundations. Notably this includes leadership of a $10 million NSF INCLUDES Alliance for Hawaii-Pacific data science that spans research, education, and workforce development efforts. She also leads a prestigious Howard Hughes Medical Institute "Inclusive Excellence" program that is focused on culture, inclusion, and belonging in STEM. She serves on the leadership teams of Hawaii's statewide NIH INBRE and NSF EPSCoR programs with specific responsibilities in faculty development and DEI. Dr. Turner has led Air Force Research Laboratory- and Air Force Office of Scientific Research-funded programs in research on nanomaterial bioeffects and training (notably ROTC and veteran upskilling in data analytics) at Chaminade for over 10 years. She is a highly regarded researcher in cellular biophysics and pharmacoanalytics, loves teaching and mentoring students, and is an advocate nationally for the potential of the Pacific and its residents to be a source of models that positively inform global change.